W9-BYG-212

He Hears the Cry of the Poor

Robert P. Maloney, C.M.

He Hears the Cry of the Poor

On the Spirituality of Vincent de Paul

New City Press

Published in the United States by New City Press
202 Cardinal Rd., Hyde Park, NY 12538
©1995 Robert P. Maloney, C. M.

Library of Congress Cataloging-in-Publication Data:

Maloney, Robert P.
   He hears the cry of the poor : on the spirituality of Vincent de
Paul / Robert P. Maloney.

   Includes bibliographical references.
   ISBN 1-56548-034-1 : $9.95
   1. Vincent de Paul, Saint, 1581-1660—Contributions in
spirituality.   2. Spirituality—Catholic Church—History—17th
century.   3. Catholic Church—Doctrines—History—17th century.
4. Church work with the poor—Catholic Church.   5. Vincentians—
Spiritual life.   6. Daughters of Charity of St. Vincent de Paul—
Spiritual life.   7. Vincentians—Rule.   8. Daughters of Charity of
St. Vincent de Paul—Rule.   I. Title.
BX4700.V6M225   1995
255'.77—dc20   95-9621

1st printing: April 1995
2d printing: November 1995

Printed in the United States of America

Contents

Introduction

For many years biblical exegesis has intrigued me. As a young priest I was sent to study biblical languages. I listened eagerly as some outstanding professors lectured about the application of literary criticism and historical criticism to the Bible. I remember how fascinated I was as I read my confrere Bruce Vawter's book, *A Path through Genesis*. It opened up a new vision of the story of creation and supplied tools that were very helpful for interpreting many other Old Testament passages. Likewise, I recall how enlightening I found the application of redaction criticism to the New Testament, examining how each of the four gospels differed from one another and discovering the varying theological perspectives through which the four evangelists expressed their faith-vision of Jesus. In more recent times, the study of hermeneutics helped me uncover new depths of meaning in the pages of the scriptures. But I recognize that all of this is insufficient.

Helpful though the interpretation of texts may be, the New Testament calls us beyond that. It invites us to enter into the world of the scriptures. I do not mean the historical world at the time of Jesus. It is impossible to enter that, nor do I suppose that many of us would want to. Rather, the scriptures invite us to enter into a "new" world. The synoptic gospels describe that world as the "reign of God." Paul speaks of living "in the Spirit." John talks of being "born from above" or of our abiding "in the Truth." In other words, the New Testament encourages us not just to apply our intellects to an understanding of the text, but to give our whole selves to a new way of being, which is inaugurated in the person of Jesus.

It is the same with studying Saint Vincent. I find the volumes of his writings very inviting. His letters are filled with good humor, wisdom, spiritual insight, and sound practical advice. His talks to the Daughters of Charity have warmth and charm. His conferences to the Missionaries vibrate with Christ-centeredness and missionary zeal.

But it is not enough to study him. Saint Vincent too holds out an alternative world to us, and he asks us to enter into it. It is a world where the poor are the masters and where we are their servants. His is a particular interpretation, and today an especially appealing one, of the world to which Jesus invites us in the gospel. It is a world where the key attitudes are simplicity, humility, and charity, and where the cross is the "royal road." It is a world where the last are first and the first are last. It is a world which, in some ways, is upside down. Saint Louise had a lovely way of putting it: "The poor person is first in the Church. He is the prince and master, being a kind of incarnation of the poor Christ. We must therefore serve him with respect, no matter what his character is like, no matter what his defects. And we must love him."[1]

May I invite you to enter into Saint Vincent's world? I speak, of course, not of the world of the seventeenth century, but rather the world where the following of Christ as the Evangelizer of the Poor is everything. In that world, values that have great importance in other "worlds"—wealth, power, sexual fulfillment, popularity, self-determination—occupy a very different position. For Christ, the Evangelizer of the Poor, they are all relativized—they pale in light of the kingdom of God. Saint Vincent calls us not merely to study about this Christ, but to enter into his mind, his vision, his sentiments, his heart. For Saint Vincent *this Christ*, the Evangelizer of the Poor, is the center of the universe. He reveals to Vincent how to relate to God and his providence, how to serve the poor, how to live daily in communion with others, how to pray.

In offering you these essays and talks, I invite you not just to read them, but to enter into the world that Saint Vincent holds out to us. He calls us to walk in the footsteps of Christ the Evangelizer of the Poor, to "put on" his simplicity, humility, gentleness, self-denial, and burning love. He calls us to give the poor first place and to allow ourselves to be their servants. "There is no better way to assure our eternal happiness," Saint Vincent tells us, "than to live and die in the service of the poor within the arms of providence and in a real renunciation of ourselves by following Jesus Christ."[2]

A few apologies. The reader will surely "catch" me when in my talks I say the same things, on different occasions, to Vincentians and Daughters of Charity. There is, of course, much in the mission, tradition, and spirituality of our Vincentian family that overlaps, even though the

---

1. J. Calvet, *Louise de Marillac par elle-même, Portrait* (Aubier, 1958) 75.
2. SV III, 392. *SV* refers to the fourteen volume French edition of Saint Vincent's works, *Correspondence, entretiens, documents*, edited by Pierre Coste (Paris: Gabalda, 1920-25).

various branches have distinct charisms. As I put together this book, I considered eliminating completely the repetitions in the second and third sections. In the end, however, I decided to leave the talks more or less as they were given, since the repetitions are not numerous and the talks were written as a single piece. I trust in the reader's understanding in this regard.

I also ask the reader's indulgence in regard to my failure to use inclusive language consistently. As is evident, some of the chapters were originally addressed exclusively to men; others, to women.

I offer this small book to all those who are seeking to give their lives to God in the service of the poor. As is evident, the later chapters were originally talks given to groups of Vincentians and Daughters of Charity, but I trust that these too might be of some help to all those who walk in the footsteps of Saint Vincent de Paul.

Abbreviations

AAS   Acta Apostolicae Sedis

C   Constitutions of the Congregation of the Mission

CR   Common Rules of the Congregation of the Mission

SV   *Vincent de Paul, Correspondence, entretiens, documents*, 14 vols., edited by Pierry Coste (Paris: Gabalda, 1920-25). All references in this book are to Coste's French edition. The translations, when they are not my own, are taken from the English edition of this work, *Vincent de Paul, Correspondence, Conferences, Documents*, vols. 1-4 (Brooklyn/Hyde Park: New City Press, 1985-   ).

SW   *Spiritual Writings of Louise de Marillac*, edited and translated from the French by Sr. Louise Sullivan, D.C. (Brooklyn: New City Press, 1991).

Some Essays
in
Vincentian Spirituality

Listening as the Foundation for Spirituality[1]

Each morning he wakes me to hear,
to listen like a disciple.
The Lord Yahweh has opened my ear.

(Isaiah 50:4-5)

Have you ever noticed how little *explicit* emphasis there is on listening in the "Rules" of communities, in the standard "manuals" on the spiritual life, and even in the classics? One searches in vain for a chapter on listening in the writings of Benedict or Ignatius, and even in the writings of very practically oriented saints like Francis de Sales and Vincent de Paul. The same is true for the writings of Luis de Granada and Rodriguez, or in later widely used treatises on spirituality like Tanquerey. It is true, of course, that listening enters the picture implicitly under many headings in these writings. But if one views listening as the foundation for spirituality, as is the thesis of this chapter, one might surely expect it to stand out in greater relief.

This chapter has a very modest goal. It proposes to offer some preliminary reflections on listening as the foundation of spirituality. I say "preliminary" reflections because all of the headings below could be much further developed, as will be evident to the reader. In fact, the author would hope that various readers, working from their own fields of expertise (philosophical, biblical, theological, as well as those of various religious congregations) might develop this thesis more fully.

To undergird and then concretize the thesis, the chapter will examine, in a preliminary way: 1) listening in the New Testament (Luke's gospel); 2) listening as the basis for spirituality; 3) some echoes of the theme in the Vincentian tradition; 4) the contrast between an implicit and an explicit theme; 5) some ramifications today.

---

1. Article originally published in *Vincentiana* 3 (Rome: Curia Generalitia, 1992); modified version published in *Review for Religious*, vol. 51, n. 5, 659-74.

13

Listening in Luke's Gospel

A broader investigation of the question would, of course, begin with the Old Testament, where the listening theme plays a vital role, especially in the Deuteronomic and prophetic traditions. There, Yahweh frequently complains that while he speaks his people "do not listen." Conversely, the prophets are pre-eminent listeners; they hear what Yahweh has to say and then speak in his name. "Speak, Lord, for your servant is listening" (Sam 3:10), says the boy Samuel as he begins his prophetic career.

The listening theme likewise recurs again and again in the New Testament, where a study of Johannine literature, for instance, would reveal listening as the key to eternal life. "Whoever is of God listens to every word God speaks. The reason you do not hear is that you are not of God. . . . If someone is true to my word, he shall never see death" (Jn 8:47, 51).

Here, however, I will offer just a brief analysis of Luke's gospel, where the listening theme is quite explicit. For Luke, as for the entire New Testament, God takes the initiative through his word, which breaks into the world as good news; listening is the indispensable foundation for all human response to that word.

Mary, the model listener

As with almost all the important themes in Lucan theology, the listening theme is introduced in the infancy narratives. These narratives, by way of preface, provide a summary of the theology that Luke will weave through his gospel. The listening theme is among the most prominent Lucan motifs (parenthetically, one might add that in Luke's gospel another theme is at work in many of the listening stories, since, contrary to the expected cultural patterns of the writer's time, a *woman* is the model listener presented to the reader).

Mary is evangelized in Luke's opening chapters. She is the first to hear the good news. She is the ideal disciple, the model for all believers. In the infancy narratives, Mary listens reflectively to:

> **Gabriel,** who announces the good news of God's presence and tells her of the extraordinary child whom she is to bear (Lk 1:26f);

Elizabeth, who proclaims her blessed among women, because she has believed that the word of the Lord would be fulfilled in her (Lk 1:39f);

Shepherds, who tell her and others the message which has been revealed to them about the child, the good news that a Savior is born! (Lk 2:16f);

Simeon, who proclaims a canticle and an oracle: the first, a song of praise for the salvation that has come to all the nations; the second, a prophecy that ominously forebodes the scandal of the cross (Lk 2:25f);

Anna, who praises God in Mary's presence and keeps speaking to all those who are ready to hear (Lk 2:36f);

Jesus himself, who tells her about his relationship with his heavenly Father, which must take precedence over everything else (Lk 2:41f).

Mary's attitude of attentiveness

When the word of God breaks in on Mary's life, she listens attentively. Using a standard pattern, Luke pictures Mary as listening to the word with wonderment, questioning what it might mean, deciding to act on it, and then meditating on the mystery of God's ways.

Listening: "Upon arriving, the angel said to her: 'Rejoice, O highly favored daughter! The Lord is with you'" (Lk 1:28).

Being astonished: "She was deeply troubled by his words, and wondered what his greeting meant" (Lk 1:29).

Questioning: "How can this be since I do not know man?" (Lk 1:34).

Acting (accepting, obeying): "Be it done to me according to your word" (Lk 1:38).

Treasuring and pondering: "Mary treasured all these things and reflected on them in her heart" (Lk 2:19, 51).

Stories of discipleship

Luke uses three brief stories to illustrate this central discipleship theme: namely, that it is those who listen to the word of God and act on it who are the true followers of Jesus.

> His mother and brothers came to be with him, but they could not reach him because of the crowd. He was told, "Your mother and your brothers are standing outside and they wish to see you." He told them in reply, "My mother and my brothers are those who listen to the word of God and act upon it." (Lk 8:19-21)

In this story, Luke changes the Markan emphasis radically (cf. Mk 3:31-35). While Mark depreciates the role of Jesus' mother and relatives, Luke extols it (echoing Luke 1:38; 2:19; 2:51): Jesus' mother is the ideal disciple, who listens to God's word and acts on it. Anyone who does likewise will be happy.

> On their journey Jesus entered a village where a woman named Martha welcomed him to her home. She had a sister named Mary, who seated herself at the Lord's feet and listened to his words. Martha, who was busy with all the details of hospitality, came to him and said, "Lord, are you not concerned that my sister has left me to do the household tasks all alone? Tell her to help me." The Lord in reply said to her: "Martha, Martha, you are anxious and upset about many things; one thing only is required. Mary has chosen the better portion and she shall not be deprived of it." (Lk 10:38-42)

Even though Jesus' statement about the one thing necessary has been subject to innumerable interpretations, there is little doubt about the central point of this story in the context of Luke's gospel. Mary has chosen the better part because she is sitting at Jesus' feet and listening to his words, just as any true disciple does. While there are many other themes in the story (such as, once again, the role of women, and also the role of the home-church in early Christianity, which is reinforced here through a Lucan addition), Luke again emphasizes what ultimately grounds the following of Jesus: listening to the word of God. That is the better part (cf. Lk 8:4-21).

While he was saying this a woman from the crowd called out, "Blessed is the womb that bore you and the breasts that nursed you!" "Rather," he replied, "blest are they who listen to the word of God and keep it." (Lk 11:27-28)

This passage interrupts, rather puzzlingly, a series of controversies that Jesus is involved in during the journey to Jerusalem. But Luke inserts it here as an occasion for Jesus to clarify the true meaning of discipleship once more: real happiness does not lie in physical closeness to Jesus, nor in blood relationship with him, but in listening to the word of God and acting on it.

Listening as the Basis for Spirituality

All spirituality revolves around self-transcendence. As a working definition for spirituality, we might use one proposed by Sandra Schneiders, who defines it as "the experience of consciously striving to integrate one's life in terms not of isolation and self-absorption but of self-transcendence toward the ultimate value one perceives."[2]

In the Christian context, spirituality involves "putting on the Lord Jesus Christ" (Rom 13:14), "giving away one's life rather than saving it up" (Mk 8:35; Mt 16:25; Lk 9:24; Jn 12:25), and other phrases that imply self-transcendence. The self is not obliterated through self-transcendence; rather, it becomes fully actualized.[3] That is the Christian paradox: in giving oneself, one finds one's true self. In that sense, authentic love of God, of neighbor, and of self come together.

Different contemporary authors put this in different ways. For Bernard Lonergan, self-transcendence occurs in the radical drive of the human spirit, which yearns for meaning, truth, value, and love. Authenticity then "results from long-sustained exercise of attentiveness, intelligence, reasonableness, responsibility."[4] For Karl Rahner, the human person is the

---

2. Sandra Schneiders, "Spirituality in the Academy," *Theological Studies* 50 (1989) 684.
3. Cf. Gal 2:19-21: "I have been crucified with Christ, and the life I live now is not my own; Christ is living in me. Of course, I still live my human life, but it is a life of faith in the Son of God, who loved me and gave himself for me." The Greek text identifies Jesus as the "self-giving one." It also makes it clear that self-transcendence does not wipe out true humanity, but fulfills it.
4. Bernard Lonergan, *A Third Collection*, edited by Frederick Crowe (New York: Paulist Press, 1985) 9.

event of the absolute self-communication of God. In his foundational works, Rahner describes the human person as essentially a listener, one who is always awaiting a possible word of revelation. Only in Jesus, the self-communication of God, is the human person ultimately fulfilled. At the core of the historical human person is a gnawing hunger for the other, for absolute value. A particular spirituality is a way in which this longing for the absolute is expressed.[5]

But this inner yearning for truth and love, this "reaching out," as Henri Nouwen expresses it, can only be satisfied by a word from without—spoken or enfleshed—that reveals the meaning of what true humanity really is. In the human person the fundamental disposition for receiving that word or Word is listening.

It is worth noting here that the Book of Genesis, wisdom literature, and the Johannine tradition all seize on the concept of the "Word" as the way in which God initiates and breaks into human history. The creating word bears within it its own immediate response: "Let there be light, and there was light" (Gn 1:3). But the word spoken to the human person, who in God's image and likeness rules with freedom over all creation, must be listened to and responded to freely.

Of course, listening here is used in the broadest sense. It includes seeing, hearing, sensing, feeling, perceiving. "Attentiveness" might serve as an umbrella term that encompasses the various ways in which the human person is open to grasp what comes from without. Listening in this sense is the indispensable pre-condition for self-transcendence. Without it, the word that comes from without goes unheard, the truth that draws the human mind to a vision that goes beyond itself goes unperceived, the love that seeks to capture the heart goes unrequited.

Is this why the saints have so stressed the importance of listening in prayer? Is this why obedience has played such an influential role in the tradition of religious communities? Is this why the seeking of counsel has always been regarded as one of the signs of true wisdom? Is this why the Word-made-flesh and the word of God in the scriptures are at the center of all Christian spirituality? Is this why the reading of the scriptures at the Eucharist and communion with the Word himself in his self-giving, sacrificial love are "the source and summit" of genuine Christian living?

---

5. Cf. K. Rahner, *Grundkurs des Glaubens* (Freiburg: Herder, 1984) 35f.; 42f.

Some Echoes of the Theme
in the Vincentian Tradition

The central place of listening, within the context of spirituality, is not explicit in the conferences and writings of Saint Vincent. But the spirituality proposed by Saint Vincent includes several key themes in which the importance of listening is evident.

Humility as the foundation of evangelical perfection

Vincent calls humility "the foundation of all evangelical perfection and the core of the spiritual life."[6] For him, the humble person, on the deepest level, sees everything as gift. The humble recognize that God is seeking to enter their lives again and again so that he might speak to them. So they are alert, they listen for God's word, they are eager to receive God's saving love. The humble know that the truth which sets them free comes from without: through God's word, through the cries of the poor, through the Church, through the community they live in.

There is probably no theme that Saint Vincent emphasized more. He described humility as the origin of all the good that we do (SV IX, 674; cf. CR II, 7). He told the Daughters of Charity: "If you establish yourselves in it, what will happen? You will make of this Company a paradise, and people will rightly say that it is a group of the happiest people on earth" (SV X, 439).

Humility and listening are closely allied, in that listening is the basic attitude of those who know that fullness of life, salvation, wisdom, truth, love, come from without. Brother Robineau, Vincent's secretary, whose reflections about the saint have just been published, notes that this attitude was especially evident in Vincent's conversations with the poor, with whom he would sit and converse with great friendliness and humility.[7]

Saint Vincent loved to call the poor the real "lords and masters" (cf. SV IX, 119; X, 332) in the Church. It is they especially who must be listened to and obeyed. In the reign of God, the world of faith, they are the kings and queens, we are the servants. Recognizing the special place of the poor

---

6. *Common Rules of the Congregation of the Mission* II, 7; henceforth CR.
7. *Monsieur Vincent raconté par son secrétaire*, edited by André Dodin (Paris: O.E.I.L., 1991), cf. #s 46 and 54.

in the new order established by Jesus, the contemporary Vincentian heritage urges that the followers of Saint Vincent, like the founder, be "always attentive to the signs of the times and the more urgent calls of the Church,"[8] "so that not only will we attend to their evangelization (that of the poor), but that we ourselves may be evangelized by them" (C 12, 3°).

Reading sacred scripture

Saint Vincent was convinced that the word of God never fails. It is like "a house built upon rock" (CR II, 1). He therefore begins each chapter of his rule, and many individual paragraphs, with a citation from scripture. He asks that a chapter of the New Testament be read by each member of his community every day. Basically, he wants them to listen to the word of God and to make it the foundation of all they do:

> Let each of us accept the truth of the following statement and try to make it our most fundamental principle: Christ's teaching will never let us down, while worldly wisdom always will.
> (CR II, 1)

In a colorful passage, Abelly notes how devoted Saint Vincent was to listening to the word of God: "He seemed to suck meaning from passages of the scriptures as a baby sucks milk from its mother, and he extracted the core and substance from the scriptures so as to be strengthened and have his soul nourished by them—and he did this in such a way that in all his words and actions he appeared to be filled with Jesus Christ."[9]

In a conference on the "Gospel Teachings," given on February 14, 1659, Vincent emphasizes how well Mary listened to the word of God. "Better than anyone else," he states, "she penetrated its substance and showed how it should be lived" (SV XII, 129).

"Obeying" everyone

The word "obedience" (*ob* + *audire* = to listen thoroughly) is related etymologically to the word "listen" (*audire*). For Saint Vincent the role

---

8. *Constitutions of the Congregation of the Mission* 2; henceforth, C.
9. Louis Abelly, *The Life of the Venerable Servant of God Vincent de Paul*, 3 vols. (New Rochelle: New City Press, 1993) III:72-73.

of obedience in community was clearly very important. But he also extended obedience beyond its usual meaning, in which all are to obey the legitimate commands of superiors. Using a broadened notion of obedience, he encouraged his followers to listen to and obey *everyone*, so that they might hear more fully what God is saying and act on it.

> Our obedience ought not limit itself only to those who have the right to command us, but ought to strive to move beyond that. . . . Let us therefore consider everyone as our superior and so place ourselves beneath them, and even more, beneath the least of them, outdoing them in deference, agreeableness, and service. (SV XI, 69)

Obedience, moreover, is not the duty of "subjects" alone, but of superiors too. In fact, superiors should be the first to obey, by listening to the members well and by seeking counsel.

> There would be nothing more beautiful in the world, my Daughter, than the Company of the Daughters of Charity if . . . obedience flourished everywhere, with the Sister Servant the first to obey, to seek counsel, and to submit herself. (SV IX, 526)

An Implicit Theme versus an Explicit One

It is clear that listening plays a significant, even if unaccented, role in each of the themes described above. The importance of listening is not, therefore, a "forgotten truth" (to use Karl Rahner's phrase) either in the writings of Vincent de Paul or in the overall spiritual tradition; neither, however, is it a central one. Therein lie two dangers.

First, truths that remain secondary or merely implicit run the risk of being underemphasized or distorted. The danger of distortion can be illustrated by using the same themes described above.

Reading a chapter of the word of God daily can degenerate into fulfilling an obligation or studying a text, unless the importance of listening attentively retains its pre-eminent place. Of course, in a healthy spirituality that will not happen, but distortion occurs when spirituality begins to lose its focus.

Likewise, the practice of humility, when distorted, can result in subservience to the voices without and deafness to the voices within, where God also speaks. In such a circumstance, "humility" might mask lack of courage in speaking up, deficient self-confidence, or a negative self-image.

A distorted emphasis on obedience can result in a situation where "subjects" are expected to listen exclusively to superiors, no matter what other voices might say, even voices that conscience demands we listen to. Conversely, it could produce a situation where a superior protests too loudly that he only has to "listen" to the advice of others, not follow it (whereas, in such instances, it may be quite evident that he listens to almost no one but himself).

But when listening retains a place at the center, the danger of distortion is lessened. Reading the word of God, practicing humility, and obeying are seen as means for hearing what God is saying. The accent remains on attentiveness.

There is also a second danger. When the importance of listening *as such* is underemphasized, there is a subtle tendency to focus on *particular* practices to the detriment of others, or to be attentive to *certain* voices while disregarding others. For instance, a member of a community might pray mightily, seeking to discern what God is saying, but pay little attention to what a superior or spiritual director, who knows the person well, is trying to say. He or she may listen "transcendentally" or "vertically," so to speak, but show little concern for listening "horizontally." Along similar lines, a superior might, to use an example coming from the other direction, be very confident that, because of the grace of his office, God lets him know what his will is, while other (more human!) figures, by the grace of their office, are desperately trying to signify to the same superior that God is saying something quite different. The simple truth is: there are many voices to which we must listen, since God speaks to us in many ways. Some of these ways are obviously privileged, but none has an exclusive hold on the truth.

Some Ramifications

In his wonderful book on community, Dietrich Bonhoeffer wrote:

> The first service that one owes to others in the community consists in listening to them. Just as love of God begins by

listening to His Word, so the beginning of love for the brethren is learning to listen to them. It is because of God's love for us that he not only gives us his Word but also lends us his ear. So it is his work that we do for our brother when we learn to listen to him. Christians, especially ministers, so often think they must always contribute something when they are in the company of others, that this is the one service they have to render. They forget that listening can be a greater service than speaking. Many people are looking for an ear that will listen. They do not find it among Christians, because these Christians are talking where they should be listening. But he who can no longer listen to his brother will soon be no longer listening to God either, he will be doing nothing but prattle in the presence of God too. This is the beginning of the death of the spiritual life.[10]

If listening is so crucial to healthy spirituality, then how might members of communities grow in it, both as individuals and in common?

Listening as an individual

From reflection on the Church's long spiritual tradition one might glean a number of qualities that characterize good listeners. Here I will touch briefly on four, which seem to me crucial for growth in listening.

Humility

The indispensable quality for good listening is humility. It is "the foundation of all evangelical perfection, the core of the spiritual life," as Saint Vincent put it (CR II, 7). The humble person senses his or her incompleteness, his need for God and other human persons. So he listens.

Humility acknowledges that everything is gift; it sees clearly that all good things come from God. Saint Vincent writes to a priest of the Mission (probably Robert de Sergis or Lambert aux Couteaux): "Because we recognize that this abundant grace comes from God, a grace which he keeps on giving only to the humble who realize that all the good done through them comes from God, I beg him with all my heart to give you more and more the spirit of humility" (SV I, 182).

---

10. Dietrich Bonhoeffer, *Life Together* (London: SCM Press, 1954) 75.

But consciousness of one's incompleteness has a further dimension. It is not only "vertical," so to speak, but "horizontal"; we depend not only on God directly, but on God's creation around us. Truth, then, comes from listening not only to God himself, but to the human persons through whom God's presence and words are mediated to us. The hunger for truth and love that lie at the heart of the mystery of the human person is satisfied only from without. We are inherently social, living within a complex network of relationships with individuals and with society.

Prayerfulness and reflectiveness

It is only when what is heard is pondered, that its full meaning is revealed. The quest for truth, therefore, involves prayerfulness and reflectiveness. While at times one can hear God speak even in a noisy crowd, it is often only in silence that one hears the deepest voices, that one plumbs the depth of meaning. The Psalmist urges us: "Be still and know that I am God" (Ps 46:10).

The gospels, particularly Luke's, attest that Jesus turns to his Father again and again in prayer to listen to him and to seek his will. Prayer is then surely one of the privileged ways of listening. But it must always be validated by life. One who listens to "what God is telling me" in prayer, but who pays little heed to what others are saying in daily life is surely suspect. Prayer must be in continual contact with people and events, since God speaks not only in the silence of our hearts, but also (and often first of all) in the people around us.

Moreover, since prayer is a meeting with God himself, what *we* say in prayer is much less important than what God says to us. When there is too much emphasis on what *we* say or do during prayer, it can easily become a good work, an achievement, a speech, rather than a grace, a gift, a gratuitous word from God. Naturally, prayer, like all human activities, involves structures, personal discipline, persevering effort. But the emphasis must always be on the presence of the personal God, to whose word we must listen attentively, as he speaks to us the good news of his love for us and for others.

In an era when there is much noise, where the media, if we so choose, speak to us all day long, we must ask ourselves: Are we able to distinguish the voice of God among the many voices that are speaking? Is God's word able to say "new things" to us? Are we still capable of wonder? As may be evident to the reader, the word *wonder* has an etymological kinship, through German, with *wound*. Is the word of God able to wound us, to penetrate the membrane that seals us off, that encloses us within ourselves? Can it break into our consciousness and change us?

Respect for the words of human persons

It is here perhaps that the tradition was weakest. It did emphasize humility. It did accent the need to hear what God is saying and to discern his will. But it rarely focused explicitly, in the context of spirituality, on the central place of listening to other human persons.

Many contemporary documents put great emphasis on the dignity of the human person and on the importance of hearing the cries that come from his heart. *Gaudium et Spes* (particularly #s 9, 12 and 22) and *Redemptor Hominis* see the human person as the center of creation. In a slightly different context, *Centesimus Annus* puts it strikingly: "Today, the Church's social doctrine focuses especially on *man*" (#54).

Respect for the human person acknowledges that God lives in the other and that he reveals himself in and through him or her. It acknowledges that words of life come from the lowly as well as the powerful. In fact, Saint Vincent became gradually convinced that "the poor have the true religion" (SV XII, 171) and that we must be evangelized by them.

Many of the recently published texts of Brother Louis Robineau attest to Saint Vincent's deep respect for persons of all types. Robineau notes how well the saint listened to them: poor and rich, lay and clerical, peasant and royal.[11]

In this context, the process of questioning persons that is involved in the quest for truth takes on a new light. When there is deep respect for the human person, questioning involves a genuine search for enlightenment, rather than being, in some hidden way, refutation or accusation. Questioning is a tool for delving deeper, for unpeeling layers of meaning, for knowing the other person better, for digging toward the core of the truth.

As we attempt to develop increasing respect for the human person, surely we must ask some challenging questions. Are we really able to hear the cries of the poor, of the most oppressed: the women and children, who are often the poorest members of society; those discriminated against because of race, color, nationality, religion; the AIDS victims, who are

---

11. Dodin, *Monsieur Vincent*, especially #71-83.

often shunned by their families and by the physically healthy; those on the "edges of life," the helpless infants and the helpless aged, who are unable to speak up themselves? Are we able to hear the counsel given to us by others: by spiritual directors, by members of our own communities, by the documents of the Church and the Congregation? Are we sensitive to the contributions that come from other sources of human wisdom (like economics, sociology, the audio-visual media, the massive data now available in computerized form) that often speak concretely about the needs of the poor, that can help us find and combat the causes of poverty, or that can assist us in the new evangelization called for by the Church? Are we alert, "listening," to the "signs of the times": the increasing gap between the rich and the poor and the repeated call for justice made by the Church; the movement toward unity within global society, which is now accompanied by an opposite movement toward separatism and nationalism; the growth of the Church in the southern hemisphere, which contrasts with its diminishment in many places in the northern hemisphere.

Attentiveness

One of the most important signs of respect for the human person is attentiveness.

The contemporary documents of both the Vincentians and the Daughters of Charity put great emphasis on the need to be attentive. The Daughters' Constitutions see it as the prerequisite for achieving the apostolic goal of the Company: "Attentiveness, the indispensable foundation of all evangelization, is the first step toward it [the service of Christ in the poor]."[12]

The Vincentian Constitutions emphasize it in the context of community life: "We should pay close attention to the opinions and needs of each confrere, humbly and fraternally" (C 24, 3°). The *Lines of Action* reinforce this: "Mutual communication is the indispensable means for creating authentic communities. For this reason, it is recommended that the confreres sincerely and diligently seek ways and means to listen to each other and to share their successes and failures."[13]

---

12. *Constitutions of the Daughters of Charity* 2.9.
13. *Lines of Action for the Congregation of the Mission* 19, n. 1 (Rome: 37th General Assembly, 1986).

Likewise, attentiveness as one seeks counsel is of the greatest importance. Robineau relates how often Saint Vincent asked others their opinion about matters at hand, "even the least in the house." He often heard him state that "four eyes are better than two, and six better than four."[14]

Robineau relates an interesting incident in this regard:

> One day he told me graciously that we must make it our practice, when consulting someone about some matter, always to recount everything that would be to the advantage of the opposing party without omitting anything, just as if it were the opposing party itself that was there to give its reasons and defend itself, and that it was thus that consultations should be carried out.[15]

Listening in community

Meetings, along with consultations and questionnaires of various sorts, are among the primary means for listening in community.

Like most realities, meetings are "for better or for worse." Almost all of us have experienced that there are some that we find very fruitful; but there are others that we would be happy to forget about. To put it in another way, meetings can be a time of grace or a time when sin threatens grace.

Communities, like individuals, can become caught up in themselves. A healthy self-concern can gradually slip into an unhealthy self-preoccupation. Outgoing zeal can be replaced by self-centered security-seeking. Communities can be rescued from this state, in a way analogous to that of individuals, only through corporate humility,[16] a communal quest to listen to God, and communal attentiveness to the words of other.

Meetings as a time when sin threatens grace

When there is no listening, meetings create strife and division. They disrupt rather than unify. They deepen the darkness rather than focus the

---

14. Dodin, *Monsieur Vincent*, #52.
15. Dodin, *Monsieur Vincent*, #118.
16. Saint Vincent repeatedly emphasized the need for corporate humility if the Congregation is to grow. Cf. SV II, 233: "I think the spirit of the Mission must be to seek its greatness in lowliness and its reputation in the love of its abjection."

light. At meetings, much depends on the capacity of the members to listen. When listening wanes, meetings degenerate rapidly, with calamitous results.

Among the signs that sin is at work in meetings is *fighting*. When participants do not listen, there will inevitably be strife, bad feelings, disillusionment, bitterness. Fractious meetings result in *fleeing*. When participants do not listen, the group will back away from major decisions, especially those that demand some conversion; it will refuse to listen to the prophets; it will seek refuge in the *status quo*. A further consequence will be *fracturing*. When participants do not listen, badly divided splinter-groups will form; the "important" conversations will take place in the corridors rather than in the meeting hall; politics, in the worst sense, will take the place of discernment.

Meetings as an opportunity for grace

But meetings also provide us with a wonderful opportunity for listening and discernment. They enable communities to work toward decisions together, as a community. In order for this to happen, those who meet must be committed to sharing their common heritage, creating a climate of freedom for discussion, and planning courageously for the future.

Recounting the deeds of the past (thanksgiving): In meetings where God is at work, we recall our heritage in order to renew it. We listen to and retell "our story." We re-count and re-hear the deeds of the Lord in our history. We celebrate our gratitude in the Eucharist and let thanksgiving fill our hearts, because we have heard the wonderful works of the Lord. We share communal prayer and reflection because we believe that the faith of others strengthens us.

Creating a climate of freedom (atmosphere): The *atmosphere* will be grace-filled, if all are eager to listen to each other. If all arrive without hardened positions and prejudices, convinced that the group must seek the truth together, then the groundwork for the emergence of truth has already been laid.

Making decisions about the present (content): The *content*, no matter how concrete or seemingly pedestrian, will be grace-filled, if all hear the word of God together, listen to each other's reflections on that word, and make decisions on that basis. The decisions of a listening community will flow from its heritage, while developing it in light of contemporary circumstances. Concrete decisions will not merely repeat the past. Rather, discerning the core values of our heritage, they will concretize them in a new context.[17]

Planning for the future (providence): Meetings have an important role to play within God's providence. God provides for the growth of communities through wise decisions that govern their future, especially the training of the young, the ongoing formation of all members, and the care for the aging. But such decisions can be made only if the members of the community are willing to listen to the data that describes its present situation and projects its future needs. Communal decision-making, based on realistic projections, is one of the ways in which "providence" operates in community life. Failure to listen to the data—difficult though it may sometimes be to "hear" it honestly—will result in calamitous "blindness" and "deafness."

The listening individual and the listening community will surely grow, since listening is the foundation of all spirituality. To the listener come truth, wisdom, the assurance of being loved. To those who fail to listen comes increasing isolation.

Jesus, like the prophets, knew that listening was demanding and consequently often lacking. He lamented its absence: "Sluggish indeed is this people's heart. They have scarcely heard with their ears, they have firmly closed their eyes; otherwise they might see with their eyes, and hear with their ears, and understand with their hearts, and turn back to me, and I should heal them" (Mt 13:15). He also rejoiced in its presence: "But . . . blessed are your ears because they hear" (Mt 13:16).

In recent years many congregations have attempted to assist individuals, local communities, and assemblies to listen better. In workshops, much effort has been put into fostering practical listening skills. But are there ways in which communities, particularly during initial formation, can better communicate the importance of listening as foundational for growth? If listening is the foundation of all spirituality, as is the thesis of this chapter, then it is crucial for personal growth and for the vitality of all communities.

---

17. In his essays on spirituality, Karl Rahner distinguishes between "material" and "formal" imitation of Christ. In "material" imitation, one seeks to do the concrete things that Jesus did, without realizing the extent to which everything he did was influenced by his social context. In "formal" imitation, one seeks to find the core meaning of what Jesus said or did and to apply it within the changed social context.

The Cross in Vincentian Spirituality[1]

Probably no spiritual reading book has been more widely read than the *Imitation of Christ*. Over the centuries millions of priests, brothers, sisters, and lay men and women have read it and meditated on it. Saint Vincent and Saint Louise recommended it often to their followers.[2] At least until recent years, for many the daily reading of a small section of the *Imitation* was a part of life. Among its most eloquent passages are these famous words:

> Jesus has now many lovers of his heavenly kingdom, but few bearers of his cross. Many he has who are desirous of consolation, but few of tribulation. Many he finds who share his table, but few his fasting. All desire to rejoice with him, few are willing to endure anything for him. Many follow Jesus unto the breaking of bread; but few to the drinking of the cup of his passion (Luke 22:42). Many reverence his miracles; few follow the shame of his cross. Many love Jesus so long as no adversities befall them. Many praise and bless him, so long as they receive any consolation from him. But if Jesus hides himself, and leaves them but a little while, they fall either into complaining, or into dejection of mind.[3]

The gospel teaching upon which these stark words are based made a deep, lasting impression on Saint Vincent and Saint Louise. This chapter will focus on: 1) the cross in the New Testament; 2) the cross in the Vincentian tradition; 3) some problems in reflecting about the cross; 4) some reflections on the cross today.

---

1. Article originally published in *Vincentiana* 1-2 (Rome: Curia Generalitia, 1993); modified version published in *Review for Religious*, vol. 53, n. 4, 544-59.
2. Cf. SV I, 382; VI, 129; cf. also V, 297; *Spiritual Writings of Louise de Marillac*, edited and translated from the French by Sr. Louise Sullivan, D.C. (Brooklyn: New City Press, 1991) 434; henceforth, SW.
3. *Imitation of Christ*, book 2, chapter 11.

The Cross in the New Testament

The cross and the resurrection stand at the center of the good news. For the New Testament writers, Jesus *must* not escape his hour. He *must* undergo the cross if he is to enter into his glory. His followers too must take up their cross daily. But the cross of Christ, as well as that of his followers, is always viewed from the perspective of resurrection faith. The New Testament returns to the message of the cross again and again. Below I offer several of the most important texts in chronological order.

Some fundamental texts

"May I never boast about anything but the cross of Our Lord Jesus Christ. Through it the world has been crucified to me and I to the world" (Gal 6:14).

In this early letter, written to the Galatians probably around 54 A.D.,[4] Paul enters into combat with the Judaizers, who boast of their circumcision and their observance of the law. He states that no external observance (the law, dietary rules, circumcision) is important; what is important is that one be created anew in Christ. He boasts only about the power of God, who exalts human weakness in the crucified Lord. In an earlier passage of the same letter, he writes: "I have been crucified with Christ. And the life I live now is not my own; Christ is living in me. I still live my human life, but it is a life of faith in the Son of God, who loved me and gave himself for me" (2:19-20). Here and elsewhere, Paul affirms that through baptism the Christian has become identified with Christ's passion, death and resurrection. The person who lives and dies with Christ has a new source of activity at work within him, the glorified Lord, who has become a life-giving Spirit (cf. 1 Cor 15:45).

"Your attitude must be that of Christ. Though he was in the form of God, he did not deem equality with God something to be grasped at. Rather, he emptied himself and took the form of a slave, being born in the likeness of men. He was known to be of human estate, and it was thus that

---

4. For data about the dating and authorship of the texts cited, I have followed *The New Jerome Biblical Commentary*, edited by R. Brown, J. Fitzmyer, and R. Murphy (New Jersey: Prentice Hall, 1990).

he humbled himself, obediently accepting even death, death on a cross!
Because of this, God highly exalted him and bestowed on him the name
above every other name, so that at Jesus' name every knee must bend in
the heavens, on the earth, and under the earth, and every tongue proclaim
to the glory of God the Father: Jesus Christ is Lord!" (Phil 2:5-11).

Writing probably sometime between 54 and 57 A.D., Paul uses a hymn
to present a picture of the "self-emptying" Christ. This Christ becomes
one of us. He freely takes on a slave-like condition and dies the ignomini-
ous death of those who have forfeited all civic rights, crucifixion. The
self-abandoning act of Jesus receives an active response from God, who
exalts him in his resurrection as Lord of the universe. Thus, God's rule
over all creation is restored through Jesus' self-emptying.

"The message of the cross is complete absurdity for those heading for
ruin, but for us who are experiencing salvation, it is the power of God"
(1 Cor 1:18).

Addressing the Corinthians around the year 55 A.D., and knowing that
the community is being ripped apart by divisions, Paul states that the
standards of fallen humanity—the sort of power and the philosophical
speculation that the world relies on—are utterly futile. God's power and
God's wisdom are revealed in human "weakness." The power of suffering love, which human reasoning often fails to comprehend, is the genuine
strength of believers.

"It pleased God to make absolute fullness reside in him, and by means
of him, to reconcile everything in his person, both on earth and in the
heavens, making peace through the blood of his cross" (Col 1:19-20).

In this later text, written in the Pauline tradition, probably between 70 and
80 A.D., the author uses an early Christian hymn to present a cosmic
vision of Christ, who works in creation and in the Church. Where there
is discord, Christ creates peace. He is the ultimate reconciler. He in whom
the fullness of God and of God's creation dwells, hands himself over to
his Father in his dying. In doing so, he hands over with himself all
creatures in heaven and on earth.

"If anyone wants to be my follower, he must deny his very self, take
up his cross each day, and follow me. Whoever would save his life will
lose it. Whoever loses his life for my sake saves it. What does it profit

someone to gain the whole world and to lose his very soul in the process?" (Lk 9:23).

Luke's gospel, probably written in 80-85 A.D., focuses on the following of Christ. As he writes, the author continually keeps in mind not only Jesus himself, particularly in his journey to Jerusalem, but also us, the readers, the disciples who will be following Jesus on the journey. The shadow of the cross lies across the pages of Luke's "orderly account" (Lk 1:3), but it is brightened by the promise of the resurrection (cf. Lk 9:23; 14:27; 17:25; 24:7; 24:26; 24:46). The cross plays a "necessary" role in salvation history.[5] While Luke underlines the saving significance of Jesus' death strongly, his emphasis shifts subtly toward the saving power of the resurrection. Still, the tragedy and mystery of the cross loom large. Using the word "cross" in a metaphorical sense, Luke highlights the utter necessity for the disciple to deny himself, take up his cross, and follow Jesus.[6]

"Let us keep our eyes fixed on Jesus, who inspires and perfects our faith. For the sake of the joy which lay before him he endured the cross, heedless of its shame" (Heb 12:2).

This text, whose date and authorship are uncertain, is a "word of exhortation" (Heb 13:22). The author presents Jesus, who now sits at the right hand of the Father, as the model for endurance of hardship. He uses this example to encourage the recipients to persevere until the triumphant end of the race. The prospective joy of the resurrection gives new meaning to the cross.

Some fundamental ideas in these texts

These texts highlight the cross, but of course their ultimate focus is on the *person* of Jesus crucified and risen. The cross is the symbol of his complete self-giving. It is Jesus himself who is our salvation, life, and resurrection. He is the ultimate revelation of the Father's love for us. He saves his people from their sins. He is the eschatological promise. In him the human person's longing for happiness is fulfilled.

---

5. Cf. J. Fitzmyer, *The Gospel According to Luke I-IX*, in *Anchor Bible*, vol. 28 (New York: Doubleday, 1981) 220-221.

6. Cf. A. George, "Le sens de la mort de Jésus pour Luc," *Revue Biblique* 80 (1973) 186-217.

As is evident in the texts, the New Testament writers developed various theologies of the redemption, with Paul as the pioneer, so to speak. The texts present Jesus as the center of salvation history, as the fulfillment of the prophets. Because there has been a history of sin, so also is there a history of redemption. Jesus expiates the sins of the human race. He is the sacrificial lamb, offering himself in atonement for sin.

The dying of Jesus is also presented as a cosmic event. The powers of evil at work in the world are defeated. Jesus overcomes them. He wins victory over sin, sickness, and death. His Father takes the side of the crucified one by raising him from the dead.

But in reading these texts it is very important not to isolate the death of Jesus from his life.[7] The saving significance of Jesus' death is related to what he proclaimed and what was rejected. Jesus identifies with the outcast, the poor, the powerless. In his death, as in life, he is one of them. There is, therefore, a clear continuity between his way of living and his way of dying, his proclamation and his rejection. Jesus' death on the cross flows from his option for the poor and the powerless. He shows himself wonderfully free before the powerful of this world. He criticizes those who lay oppressive burdens on others. But he himself is powerless. So the oppressors, the powerful, reject him. His death by crucifixion is that of those who have no rights.

Today we often speak of christologies, and theologies of redemption, as having "ascending" and "descending" forms. The synoptics, starting with memories of the concrete events "here below" follow Jesus' ascent through his life, death and resurrection to the glory of the Father. In Johannine thought, as in much patristic and medieval christology, the starting point is "above," where the Word is with God in the beginning. Yet in all these theologies (ascending, descending, and many in-between) the focus is on the person of Jesus, whose sacrificial love moves him to lay down his life for his friends: his companions both then and now.[8]

In addition to this focus on the person of Jesus himself through the symbol of his cross, there also appears, in the texts cited above, a metaphorical use of the word "cross," stemming from the sayings of

---

7. Cf. E. Schillebeeckx, *Church* (New York: Crossroad, 1990), 124-25.
8. In passing, it might be said that Saint Vincent's christology, like that of most of his contemporaries, was decidedly on the descending side; cf. SV IX, 640: "God died for us"; cf. also XII, 264.

Jesus. In this usage, the "cross" refers to the sufferings that the followers of Jesus experience. For the faithful follower, the cross:

- means giving one's life
- is to be taken up daily
- brings greater riches than "saving up" one's life
- can be borne only through the power of Christ in us
- seems foolishness to the "world"
- involves forgiveness of sin
- creates peace
- is the source of joy and leads to joy.

The Cross in the Vincentian Tradition

In this age of hermeneutics we are increasingly conscious of how much our historical context influences us. Like all of us, Saint Vincent and Saint Louise were children of their times. In that context they were well educated, but neither was a speculative theologian. Both absorbed the "standard theology" of their era. Since they had an abundant measure of common sense, they avoided the extremes of some of their contemporaries. But like their contemporaries, both focus on the cross with little explicit reference to the resurrection. Strange as that may seem to modern ears, it is quite characteristic of seventeenth-century theology in France.

The language of symbols

Symbols often say much more than words. They express not only intellectual content, but also the deeply personal, affective undercurrents that words have trouble communicating. Saint Louise and Saint Vincent both recognized the importance of the symbol of the cross as a way of communicating the depth of God's love for us.[9]

The seal of the Daughters of Charity, used since 1643, is one of the expressions of the importance of the cross in Saint Louise's and Saint Vincent's minds. The present-day Constitutions of the Daughters describes it this way:

---

9. Naturally, the cross is not the only symbol of God's love; the heart of Jesus too expresses, with different overtones, God's love and Jesus' love for us (cf. SV XI, 291).

The seal of the Company of the Daughters of Charity represents a heart encompassed by flames, with a crucifix superimposed. It is surrounded by the motto: *CARITAS CHRISTI URGET NOS. The charity of Jesus Christ crucified*, which animates and sets afire the heart of the Daughter of Charity, *urges* her to hasten to the relief of every type of human misery. (p. 1)

The conclusions to many of Saint Louise's letters, which were often sealed with the image described above, also expressed verbally her personal devotion to the crucified Lord, employing varying wording: "I am, in the love of Jesus crucified . . ." "In his love and that of his crucified Son, I am . . ."[10]

From the correspondence, moreover, between Saint Vincent and Saint Louise, and between both founders and the two communities, it is quite evident that crucifixes played a significant role in the piety of many Daughters and Vincentians. The sisters often request them, and Saint Louise goes out of her way to obtain them.[11] Saint Vincent states that the Missionaries should never be without one (SV XI, 378).

The crucifix also plays a prominent role in the method of prayer that Saint Vincent taught, particularly to the Daughters of Charity, some of whom considered themselves too lacking in education to pray well, not knowing how to read or write.[12] He assures them that praying well has little relationship with knowing how to read and write, and encourages them to use images. "Where do you think the great Saint Bonaventure got all his wisdom?" he says to the Daughters. "In the sacred book of the cross!" (SV IX, 217). He also tells them the story of a person who complimented Saint Thomas on the beautiful thoughts he had about God, and recounts how Thomas told the admirer that he would show him his library, leading him then to his crucifix (cf. SV IX 32). He tells the Daughters that, while only some can use methods of prayer like those described in Francis de Sales' *Introduction to the Devout Life*, everyone can place herself at the foot of the cross in the presence of God. If she has nothing to say, she can wait until God speaks to her (cf. SV IX, 50).

---

10. Cf. SW 54, 325, 349, 354, 424, 439, etc.
11. Cf. SW 326, 332, 525, 530, 547, 635.
12. In this connection, one might also mention the sign of the cross, which Saint Vincent saw as a means of offering all one's actions to God (cf. SV X, 629-630). He saw it as the sign by which Christians, from ancient times, could recognize one another and a reminder of the mystery of the Trinity (cf. SV XIII, 159).

In fact, for Saint Vincent no prayer is more pleasing to God than daily meditation on the passion and death of our Lord (cf. SV X, 569).

The writings of Saint Vincent and Saint Louise

The texts in which Saint Vincent and Saint Louise speak of the cross are far too numerous to cite exhaustively. Their references to the cross, moreover, are usually made in passing, without extensive development (though Louise reflects on the cross explicitly in a brief meditation written down in her later years, cf. SW 775-76). References to the resurrection, as mentioned above, are relatively few. I offer here, in a synthetic way, a brief analysis of meaning of the cross as the two saints speak of it and write about it in very varied contexts.

The cross—symbol of God's love as revealed in Jesus

"May your love and that of Jesus Crucified be eternally exalted!" Saint Louise exclaims at the end of an Act of Consecration that she signed (SW 694).

Both saints often dwelt on God's love for us (cf. SV IX, 269). The cross is the symbol of the Father's love, as revealed in the death of his Son. In their reflections both on the cross and on the heart of Jesus, the two saints often remind their followers of how deep God's love for us is. On July 5, 1641, Saint Louise writes to Sr. Elizabeth Martin: "I beg our beloved Jesus Crucified to attach us firmly to his cross, so that we may be closely united to him by his love and that our little sufferings and the little we accomplish may be in and for his love, in which I remain, my dear Sister, your very humble sister and servant" (SW 54).

"Our Lord had to predispose with his love," Saint Vincent writes to Monsieur Portail, "those whom he wished to have believe in Him" (SV I, 295). The conviction of both Saint Vincent and Saint Louise was concrete and strong: we believe in and love those from whom we sense love. Jesus, in his dying on the cross, reveals God's love in its depths.

To be a Daughter of Charity is to be a Daughter of the Cross

Love of neighbor, and particularly service of the poor, will inevitably involve the "cross," in the metaphorical sense. In fact, to be a Daughter of Charity, a Daughter of Love (SV IX, 53; X, 459, 474), means becoming identified with the crucified Lord. Toward the end of his life, Saint

Vincent writes to Avoie Vigneron (SV VII, 241): "Receive it [this suffering] as a gift from [God's] paternal hand, and try to use it well. Help your sister to carry her cross, since yours is not as heavy as hers. Make her remember that she is a Daughter of Charity and that she ought to be crucified with our Lord and submit to his good pleasure in order not to be completely unworthy of so worthy a father." He writes to Saint Louise during one of her sicknesses: "I learned of your illness upon my return. It has saddened me. I am begging Our Lord to restore you to that perfect health which made me so happy the last time I saw you. Well, you are a daughter of the cross. Oh! what a happiness!" (SV I, 342).

In a similar way, Saint Louise recognizes that her vocation means identifying with the cross. In a reflection on charity, she writes: "God, who has granted me so many graces, led me to understand that it was his holy will that I go to him by way of the cross" (SW 711). At a much later period in her life, writing on the pure love we have vowed to God and the need to give ourselves completely to him, she states: "As proof thereof, I am going to follow you to the foot of your cross which I choose as my cloister" (SW 828).

Since there are so few explicit references to the resurrection, one could imagine this spirituality to take on rather gloomy tones. With Saint Vincent, this is not the case. He encouraged the Daughters to be joyous, smiling in the service of the poor. Sometimes, though, he had to work at counteracting a tendency toward over-seriousness in Saint Louise, encouraging her, for instance, as she was about to journey with the more ebullient Madame Goussault: "Please be very cheerful with her, even though you should have to lessen a bit that somewhat serious disposition which nature has bestowed on you and which grace is tempering by the mercy of God" (SV I, 502).

The cross and providence

Both saints have a deep devotion to providence. In the course of their lives, they become more and more convinced of God's love for them and grow in confidence that God is always at work in the events that occur, whether joyful or painful. Saint Vincent tells the missionaries in the year before his death: "My brothers, you ought to rest in the loving care of his Providence. . . . Do not trouble yourself about anything except seeking the kingdom of God, because his infinite wisdom will provide for all the rest" (SV XII, 142).[13] Both he and Saint Louise see the cross as a part of that providence.

On March 26, 1653, Saint Louise writes to Sr. Jeanne Lepintre: "It is perhaps for that reason, my dear Sister, that our Lord inspires you to remain at peace at the foot of his cross, completely submissive to the guidance of his divine providence. It seems to me, my very dear Sister, that you have found the philosopher's stone of devotion when the firm resolution to do his will calms your anxieties" (SW 416). During times of trial or calumny, both saints are quick to remind their communities that they are sharing, under God's providence, in the cross of Christ. Near the end of her life, Saint Louise writes to Sr. Françoise Carcireux: "We, however, and especially the entire Company, must accept this trial as coming from divine providence as our share in the cross of our Lord and as an opportunity he has given you to enable all of us to follow him" (SW 668). A year earlier Saint Vincent had published a similar statement in the Common Rules he gave to the Congregation of the Mission: "If divine providence ever allows a house or a member of the Congregation, or the Congregation itself, to be subjected to, or tested by, slander or persecution . . . we should ever praise and bless God, and joyfully thank him for it as an opportunity for great good, coming down from the Father of lights" (CR II, 13).

United with Christ crucified and living by the power of God

In her "Thoughts on the Cross," Saint Louise exclaims: "O Holy cross! O suffering! How amiable you are, since the love of God has given way to you in his Son to gain through you the power to give paradise to those who had lost it by pleasure!" (SW 776).[14]

It is only when one is willing to die with Christ that one finds the strength to live as his follower; conversely, it is only by living with Christ that we learn to die. "Remember, Father," Saint Vincent writes to Monsieur Portail, "that we live in Jesus Christ by the death of Jesus Christ, and that we ought to die in Jesus Christ by the life of Jesus Christ, and that our life ought to be hidden in Jesus Christ and full of Jesus Christ,

---

13. Cf. also T. Lane, "She will find them again: Musings on Saint Louise," *Colloque* 24 (Autumn 1991), 416-18, where the author also points out Saint Louise's capacity to laugh.

14. An inordinate quest for pleasure has always been one of the roots of sin, but one cannot escape noticing that Saint Louise and Saint Vincent are both affected by the rather negative attitude toward created reality (and pleasure) that affected their era.

and that in order to die like Jesus Christ it is necessary to live like Jesus Christ" (SV I, 295).

Real holiness flows from the cross, where the power of God works within us. In the midst of her worries about her son, Saint Louise asks Saint Vincent: "Do me the charity of asking our good God that, through his mercy, my son may participate one day in the merits and death of Jesus Crucified, the living source of all holiness" (SW 184).

In a touching letter to Jeanne Lepintre, she also writes: "Tell our sisters that the people of Nantes are clamoring against them more than they know, and in important matters. However, it is the evil one playing these games that he will not win, provided they gather together and unite near the cross, like chicks under their mother's wing when the owl lies in wait" (SW 213).

Saint Vincent, in speaking to the missionaries about the martyrdom of Pierre Borguny, states: "Courage, my brothers! Let us trust that our Lord will strengthen us in the crosses that come to us, great though they may be, when he sees that we love them and that we have confidence in him" (SV XI, 392).

A privileged way

Both saints were utterly convinced of this. They repeated it to each other and to their followers. In a letter written some time before 1634, Saint Vincent says to Saint Louise: "Our Lord will see to the matter, especially if you are happy at the foot of the cross where you are at present and which is the best place in this world you could be. So be happy there, Mademoiselle, and fear nothing" (SV I, 152).

In a letter that combines several of the themes described above, Saint Louise writes to Charlotte Royer, using language reminiscent of the *Imitation of Christ*, "You are well aware, my dear Sister, that the path by which God wants you to go to him is the royal road of the cross" (SW 527). She tells Srs. Catherine Baucher and Marie Donion: "Yes, my dear Sisters, the greatest honor you can receive is to follow Jesus Christ carrying his cross" (SW 535).

In her "Thoughts on the Cross," she states that "souls chosen by God are very particularly destined to suffer" (SW 775). Meditating on charity, she says of herself: "God, who has granted me so many graces, led me to understand that it was his holy will that I go to him by way of the cross.

His goodness chose to mark me with it from my birth and he has hardly ever left me, at any age, without some occasion of suffering" (SW 711).

Jesus on the cross as a means of encouraging others

The two founders experienced abundant sufferings themselves: the distress of the poor; the ravages of war; the pains of giving birth to two new communities; the difficulties in community life as the years went on; criticism from within and from outside their communities; their own interior struggles; sickness; the death of their closest friends; their own dying. They bore these crosses as part of God's providence.

But they also recognized that not every "cross" should be carried, since sometimes the sufferings involved could be remedied. Saint Louise, for example, writes to Sr. Elizabeth Brocard, a new sister servant: "If some little cause for suffering arises, humble yourself and accept it as a cross to be cherished because our Lord has permitted you to bear it. This does not mean, my dear Sister, that if your sufferings continue, you should not make them known to us or that we will not make every effort to meet your needs" (SW 449).

Other crosses should be borne with courage, since to lay them aside would cause greater pain for others. "It is much better to love one's distress when one experiences it," Saint Louise writes to Joan Lepintre, "and carry it to the foot of the cross, or to let the Sister Servant know of it, than to look for a way to be rid of it that could cost so dearly" (SW 269).

The cross comes up especially when Saint Vincent and Saint Louise speak about illness. Writing to Françoise Carcireux about the sickness that Sr. Charlotte Royer was suffering, Saint Louise states: "Our Lord may use them [her ailments] to sanctify her by the merits of his holy life and his precious death for us upon the cross" (SW 526). In describing the death of Barbe Angiboust, she writes: "During her illness, God honored her by the most excellent marks of a true Christian woman and servant of God by granting her the grace to conform her will to his, to raise her thoughts frequently to Jesus Crucified and to practice great patience" (SW 629).

Some Problems in Reflecting About the Cross

The Jews and Gentiles have not been alone in finding the cross a "stumbling block" and "foolishness." On the theological level, there have always been difficulties in dealing with the cross, and more generally with the problem of evil.

Some of the difficulties in developing a theology of the cross stem from differences in the way of perceiving God.[15] Both the Jewish and Christian scriptures praise God under two aspects. On the one hand, he is above all creation, utterly transcendent. On the other hand, he is intimately involved with his creatures and feels their afflictions: God suffers in pain for his people.[16]

When Christianity moved out into the Hellenistic world, it encountered a Greek conception of God that did not easily enter into a peaceful union with the immanent aspect of God's presence in the scriptures: The Greek God was totally self-contained, world-transcending, incapable of being touched by human action or suffering. Consequently, the marriage between the immanent aspect of the biblical view of God and the Greek concept of God has had a rocky history. By the time of the great scholastics the Greek view exercised a predominant influence: God as God cannot suffer; God suffers only in the humanity of Jesus. How different this is from the view of Hosea for whom God's bowels tremble with compassion as he decides not to give rein to the heat of his anger (cf. Hos 11:8).

But many modern minds and hearts find the Greek-influenced scholastic view difficult to accept. It seems to place God at a great distance from those who suffer. In the 1940s, shortly before his death, Dietrich Bonhoeffer wrote that "only a suffering God can help." In the 50s Jacques Maritain stated: "We need to integrate suffering with God, for the idea of an insensitive and apathetic God is revolting to the masses." In the '60s and '70s a series of essays by Karl Rahner further explored the question.

---

15. For a very good treatment of contemporary christology, and its historical roots, cf. Elizabeth Johnson, *Consider Jesus* (New York: Crossroad, 1990), especially chapter 8 on "God and the Cross"; also, K. Rahner, "On the Theology of the Incarnation," *Theological Investigation* IV (London: Darton, Longman, and Todd, 1966), 105-20; also, K. Rahner, *Sacramentum Mundi* II (London: Burns and Oates, 1969), 207f.

16. One might cite many texts indicating God's feelings in regard to his people; cf. Gen 6:6; Jos 24:19; Hos 11:8; Is 42:14; Ps 103.

In the 80s both sides of the problem were given clear, forceful presentations in Jürgen Moltmann's *The Crucified God* and Edward Schillebeeckx's books *Jesus* and *Christ*. Moltmann seeks to articulate a theology of a suffering God. God suffers, Moltmann holds, not out of a deficiency in his divine nature, but because he freely chooses to be affected by what affects others. Schillebeeckx, on the other side, in an approach closer to the classical tradition, holds that God does not suffer. Rather, he resists evil in Jesus and is in solidarity with those who suffer, overcoming suffering through his compassionate presence. This presence is mediated "sacramentally" in Jesus and in those who, sharing Jesus' life, resist injustice.[17]

Whatever side of the debate one might sympathize with, out of all this literature has flowed another title for Jesus, "Jesus, the Compassion of God."[18]

On a theoretical-practical level, there is a perennial danger, by no means absent today, that the cross might sometimes be used as ideology, that is, as an argument for justifying oppressive behavior. In an unjust society, for example, it can be used as a tool to motivate the poor to accept injustice silently.

In the years following the Medellin conference in 1968, a strong critique developed among theologians, particularly in Latin America, about the role theology and popular piety have played in supporting situations of injustice. Might not an over-emphasis on the crucified, dead Christ, who has gone meek as a lamb to the slaughter, legitimate suffering as the will of God? Does it not cultivate a mentality that says: accept the cross meekly and you will receive eternal life? And does this not work to the advantage of the oppressor?

Quite on the contrary, Christians must labor for the well-being of all and for liberation from structures that favor the few over the many, the rich over the poor, one racial, social or religious group over others. In fact, liberation from oppression is one of the signs of the kingdom. The Christian cannot, therefore, stand by in silence in the face of injustice.

---

17. Cf. Johnson, *Consider Jesus*, 119; also E. Schillebeeckx, *Christ: The Experience of Jesus as Lord* (New York: Crossroad, 1980), 728f.; J. Moltmann, *The Crucified God: The Cross of Christ as the Foundation and Criticism of Christian Theology* (New York: Harper and Row, 1974).
18. Cf. Monica Hellwig, *Jesus, the Compassion of God* (Wilmington: M. Glazier, 1985).

Rather, he must be willing to suffer for justice's sake. While one must certainly distinguish between material progress and the advent of the kingdom of God, nonetheless the life of the kingdom, already at work in believers, moves the Christian to work to "bring glad tidings to the poor, to proclaim liberty to captives, recovery of sight to the blind, and release to prisoners" (Lk 4:18).[19]

Unfortunately, oppressive ideologies can be present not only in civil society but in the Church and religious life as well. "Acceptance" can be eulogized rather than constructive criticism. Voices that call for repentance or needed changes can be marginalized or silenced.

3. There is a third problem that can arise on the personal, ascetical level: that of distortion in the practice of asceticism. In the Vincentian tradition, self-imposed "crosses" are always to be used in moderation (cf. CR X, 15); they must always be seen as a function of one's apostolic and community goals. They should help us to serve the poor well, to live together well, to pray well.

It was clear to Saint Vincent and Saint Louise that life's most important "crosses" need not be constructed. They impose themselves. This is not to say that there is no place for personal discipline and for wisely-chosen practices that involve us in self-denial in order to reach the goals set before us. It is to say, however, that self-imposed mortifications must be tailored to the vocation of members of apostolic societies.

Some Reflections on the Cross Today

From what has been written above, I trust that it is evident that "devotion to the cross" is not merely an optional "private devotion" or a "personal ascetical practice."[20] Rather, it touches on the core of the good news, since the cross is the symbol of Jesus' saving love.[21]

---

19. Cf. *Gaudium et Spes* #s 39, 43, 57.
20. In a similar way, Karl Rahner, in various articles in *Theological Investigations* often argues that devotion to the Sacred Heart (symbol of God's love) is indispensable. Cf. "Behold This Heart: Preliminaries to a Theology of Devotion to the Sacred Heart" (III, 321-30); "Some Theses for a Theology of Devotion to the Sacred Heart" (III, 331-52); "The Theological Meaning of the Veneration of the Sacred Heart" (VIII, 217-28); "Unity-Love-Mystery" (VIII, 229-47); "Devotion to the Sacred Heart Today" (XXIII, 117-28).
21. Some forms of devotion to the cross are, of course, quite "private." A devotion like the "Stations of the Cross," for instance, is just one means of focusing on the cross of Christ, and is therefore quite optional.

The historical reality of the cross is at the center of revelation; it is the "sacrament" of God's love for the world and of the fullness of human response to that love.[22] The cross of Christ, therefore, stands not at the periphery of Christian life, where it might be listed among a series of devotions; rather, it stands at the very core of the creed: "He suffered under Pontius Pilate, was crucified, died, and was buried. He descended into hell. The third day he rose again from the dead."

The symbol of the cross, so central to the good news, speaks to our age, as to every age, but with different concretizations. It says forcefully to us at least the following:

1. *The crucified Jesus, in his suffering love, stands at the center of our faith, raised up by the Father, fully alive.*

The author of the first letter to Timothy tells us that the fullness of the truth lies in "the man Christ Jesus, the self-giving one" (1 Tim 2:5-6). All Christian spirituality, therefore, focuses on the crucified and risen Jesus. He is the way, the truth, and the life. No one comes to the Father except through him.

The cross is the symbol of what is at the core of Jesus' person: "The way we came to understand love was that he laid down his life for us; we too must lay down our lives for our brothers" (1 Jn 3:16). The crucified Jesus proclaims that self-giving love is at the heart of being God and at the heart of being human. "God's love was revealed in our midst in this way: he sent his only Son to the world that we might have life through him. Love, then, consists in this: not that we have loved God but that he has loved us and has sent his Son as an offering for our sins. Beloved, if God has loved us so, we must have the same love for one another" (1 Jn 4:9-11).

Nothing will nourish the missionary or the Daughter of Charity more than focusing on God's love, of which the cross is the symbol. The Missionary's personal experience of this love will move him to proclaim it as good news. The Daughter of Charity's personal experience of this love will move her to share it as healing.

The love that Jesus reveals through the symbol of the cross is:

– self-giving
– sacrificial

---

22. K. Rahner, "The Christian Understanding of Redemption," *Theological Investigations* XXI, 250.

- forgiving
- healing
- unifying
- loyal to one's friends
- powerless
- in solidarity with the weak
- confident in the power of God.

In our Vincentian context, frequent meditation on the cross, as the symbol of God's love for us and of our love for God, has abiding importance. Let me suggest the meditative use of the following texts, which refer either explicitly or implicitly to the cross and which focus on God's love for us as revealed in the person of Jesus: John 3:16-17; John 13:1-17; 1 John 4:9-10; Ephesians 1:3-14; James 1:17-18; Luke 9:23. As is evident from the texts, in the New Testament the cross is much more than an example.[23] It speaks of God's ways. It discloses the depths of his love. It proclaims that the power of God will prevail over what sinful men and women conspire to do. It reveals that true wisdom lies not with the forces of evil, but in suffering love. It initiates us into the mystery of the resurrection.

2. *All Missionaries, all Daughters of Charity—all persons—will suffer.*

Of course, some sufferings can, and should, be avoided. But the exceptionless rule of human existence, and of the following of Christ, is that there is inevitable suffering and death. The famous words of Dietrich Bonhoeffer, written prophetically a few years before his execution, capture the reality very starkly: "When Christ calls a person, he bids him come and die."[24]

Jesus' dying love gives meaning to the many "crosses" his followers are called to bear. In the life of a Missionary and a Daughter of Charity, therefore, let me suggest that the cross today, in the following of Christ, may take the following forms especially:

- laboring daily, and perseveringly, in the service of the poor
- sharing the helplessness and pain of the marginalized[25]
- standing with the abandoned and suffering in solidarity with them for justice sake[26]

---

23. Cf. Jaroslav Pelikan, *Jesus through the Centuries* (New York: Harper and Row, 1985) 105.
24. D. Bonhoeffer, *Cost of Discipleship* (New York: Macmillan, 1959) 99.
25. SV XI, 341; cf. XII, 270: "It [charity] brings it about that one cannot see anyone suffer without suffering with him; one cannot see him weeping without weeping too."
26. Cf. SV V, 545: "It is a good sign when you suffer for justice sake."

- witnessing to gospel values in a non-supportive context
- accepting events that displease us, but that we can do nothing about
- sharing some of the privations of the poor[27]
- bearing sickness, our own and that of others
- coming to grips with aging
- enduring the death of friends
- experiencing one's own dying.

Confronting inevitable suffering and death has always been, and will always be, a formidable task. But in an age that creates expectations of immediate gratification, the challenge becomes all the more difficult. Hard as it may be to accept—and though one may put this same truth in much more positive terms—dying is the focus of Christian spirituality, dying in order that one might live. One may surely dispute, in examining the *Imitation of Christ* whether certain concrete practices described in the New Testament can be demanded of each Christian (going into the desert, spending the night in prayer, Jesus' actual way of practicing poverty), but this proposition is certain: "Every Christian, at all times, follows Jesus by dying with him; following Jesus has its ultimate truth and reality and universality in the following of the Crucified."[28]

The following of the crucified Lord is the supreme act of faith; it is a surrender in hope and love into the incomprehensible mystery of God.[29]

3. *The crucified Lord suffers in "crucified persons" and in the "crucified peoples."*

Sin continues to work in our times, crucifying the Lord of history (cf. Heb 6:6). The Vincentian and the Daughter of Charity see the crucified every day. But it is easy for the "world" to forget them: the 5.7 million

---

27. Cf. SV XI, 76-77: Abelly relates that Saint Vincent remarked, in a discourse to the Missionaries, that they would be very happy if they became poor through having practiced charity towards their neighbor. Saint Vincent continued: "If God should permit them to be reduced to the necessity of going to serve as curates in villages in order to earn a living, or even if some of them were compelled to beg for their bread or sleep in rags frozen with the cold under a hedge, and if, in such a condition, a person were to ask them: 'Poor priests of the Mission, what has reduced you to this extremity?' what happiness, my brothers, if they were able to reply: 'It was charity.' Oh! how that poor priest would be esteemed before God and his angels."
28. K. Rahner, "The Following of the Crucified," *Theological Investigations* XXII, 160.
29. *Ibid.*, 168.

people of Haiti, who have been so poor for so long that their plight is no longer news; the 2.5 million Bosnian refugees who are victims of "ethnic cleansing"; the 1.5 million Somalians on the edge of death by starvation.[30] The challenge is to recognize the disfigured, crucified Lord and, like Saint Vincent and Saint Louise, to raise the consciousness of others to their plight. Contemplation of the crucified Lord cannot remain merely a pious exercise; nor can it be simply meditation on a past event. The Lord lives on in his members. He is crucified in individual persons and in suffering peoples. The call is to see him and serve him there.

One of the great gifts of the two founders was the ability to recognize Christ in the face of the suffering and to mobilize the energies of others in the service of their service. They were extraordinary organizers. To aid the most abandoned of their time, they gathered together rich and poor, women and men, clergy and laity.

They knew, to use the eloquent phrase of Jon Sobrino, that the "crucified peoples" bring salvation to us, as we labor to take them down from the cross.[31]

4. *We are evangelized by the cross, and we evangelize by the cross.*

Jesus' dying love is at the center of the good news. It is the source of our deepest hope. He laid down his life for his friends—for us!

The cross, in the New Testament, is always seen in light of the resurrection. Without the resurrection, the cross remains darkness. But, equally in New Testament faith, there is no resurrection without the cross. The cross of Christ, therefore, stands with the resurrection at the center of the good news we believe in. Together, they tell us how deeply God loves us. They evangelize us.

Yet, besides the cross of Jesus, the crosses of his members can evangelize us, too. Our lives can be transformed by the suffering love of Jesus' followers, who fill up his sufferings in their bodies: the sick, who bear illness with courage; the grieving, who hope against hope; the dying, who clearly trust in the resurrection.

And does not Jesus evangelize us through other, more "anonymous" crosses: the anguish of the starving in Africa, the deaths of countless martyrs and *desaparecidos* in Latin America, the loneliness of AIDS victims or street-people, the pain and abandonment of the elderly? Do not

---

30. Cf. *America*, vol. 167, n. 8 (September 26, 1992) 179.
31. Cf. "Los pueblos crucificados, actual siervo sufriente de Yahvé," in Jon Sobrino and Ignacio de Senillosa, *América, 500 años* (Barcelona: Cristianisme i Justícia, 1991) 28-36.

these crosses, too, call us outside ourselves to solidarity with the suffering? Do they not proclaim to us that the heart of the gospel lies in compassionate love for the most abandoned? Do they not draw us out of our isolation toward self-giving love?

The "crucified peoples" have much to teach us: pardon for their oppressors, hope in seemingly hopeless circumstances, willingness to share the little they have, gratitude for the presence and support of others, and, in the words of the Latin American Bishops' document at Puebla, "solidarity, service, simplicity, readiness to receive the gift of God" (#1147). They evangelize us from the cross.

It is only when we have been evangelized by the cross that we, too, can evangelize by preaching the message of the cross. The "foolishness" of the cross will be credible on our lips only if we have learned its "wisdom" from sharing in the suffering of our brothers and sisters.

Have we learned to preach the cross without sounding hollow? Do our lives say that the cross has meaning? Do we find simple, clear words that encourage the suffering, or gestures that console the afflicted?

5. *Within this much larger context, the self-imposed "crosses" that we often call "mortifications" play a functional, and sometimes important, role.*

From a theological perspective, today we recognize, perhaps more than ever (though a long theological tradition has already expressed this truth in varying ways), that death does not coincide completely with a final medical declaration. Dying occurs gradually throughout life; it only reaches its completion at the end (and even there its precise occurrence is difficult to define). It was natural, therefore, that Christian piety, especially as it recognized that few would actually literally be "crucified with Christ," should seek to live out the following of the crucified Christ in life.

Consequently, Christian spirituality has acknowledged from the beginning that the heroic bearing of inevitable suffering is equivalent to bearing the cross of Christ. We die with Christ little by little, in installments, so to speak. The concrete challenge, therefore, is this: Since these sufferings prefigure our death, are we able to "abandon with resignation what is taken from us, accept twilight as promise of an eternal Christmas full of light"?[32]

Other "crosses" are taken on voluntarily, or at least more or less so,

---

32. K. Rahner, "The Following of the Crucified," *Theological Investigations* XXII, 170.

for a variety of ascetical reasons which cannot be treated at length here.[33] Saint Vincent and Saint Louise both recognized the value of such practices, while warning their followers that they must always be used with discernment and moderation.

The goal of such practices is to help the Missionary or the Daughter of Charity live a fuller life by "dying" and therefore "living" more fully. As Margaret Miles puts it, "The real point of ascetic practices, then, was not to 'give up' objects, but to reconstruct the self." They should always have a positive reference point, like growth in service of the poor, community living, prayer. Examples of these might be:

Ascetical Practice	Goal
being ready to respond to the needs of the poor, particularly in accepting assignments; being willing to go even to foreign lands in their service	Service of the Poor
being faithful to the duties of one's state in life by giving preference to them when they conflict	Service of the Poor Human Maturity
with other more pleasurable things working hard as servants do	Service of the Community Service of the Poor Service of the Community
rising promptly in the morning to praise God and to support our brothers and sisters in prayer	Prayer Community Support
being sparing in obtaining or accepting material possessions	Service of the Poor Personal Freedom
being disciplined in eating and drinking; eating what is set before us; not complaining about food	Human Maturity Physical Health
employing moderation and a critical sense in using television, radio, movies, and other media	Service of the Poor Human Maturity
being slow to ask for privileges or exceptions from reasonable communal norms	Life Together
seeking to be with those who are less pleasing to us as well as with those to whom we are more attracted	Life Together
giving generously of our time in order to take part in contemporary decision-making processes withholding negatively critical and divisive words	Life Together Life Together Human Maturity

---

33. For a very interesting treatment of this question see Margaret Miles, *Practicing Christianity* (New York: Crossroad, 1988) 94-104.

In an age when scientific proof and experiential data are much emphasized, and in a climate where quick, satisfying results are much sought after, the cross is surely "foolishness." But has it not always been so? For the Christian the challenge is an abiding one: Our faith places us "at the foot of the cross," to use the phrase Saint Louise liked so well. Surely, that is the reason why the saints have so often recommended meditation on the cross as a source for growth in the spiritual life.

Is the cross, viewed from the perspective of resurrection faith, still the nourishment that vivifies us today, as it did our founders? Is it a rich grace-giving font for our spirituality?

The message of the cross will always be difficult to hear, even for the messengers who proclaim it. While it is good news when viewed from the light of resurrection faith, it costs dearly when lived out daily. It is life-giving, but its life comes through death. It stands at the center of Christian faith, yesterday and today.

> How precious the gift of the cross, how splendid to contemplate![34]

---

34. From a sermon by Saint Theodore the Studite; *Patrologia Graeca* 99:691.

Providence Revisited[1]

Lead, kindly Light, amid the encircling gloom,
Lead thou me on. . . .
Keep thou my feet; I do not ask to see
The distant scene; one step enough for me.

John Henry Newman

Throughout his life, Saint Vincent spoke of providence with great conviction. He saw God's plan at work everywhere. He invoked providence to encourage those who found themselves groping in the darkness, to strengthen those experiencing pain, to slow down the hasty, to promote initiative in those planning the future.

This chapter will attempt: 1) an analysis of providence in the words, writings, and life of Saint Vincent; 2) a description of some fundamental shifts that have taken place in thinking between the seventeenth and twentieth centuries; 3) a "re-visiting" of providence today; 4) a parable.

Providence in Saint Vincent

As one reads Saint Vincent, it becomes utterly clear how important a role providence plays for him. At times his words are eloquent:

> We cannot better assure our eternal happiness than by living and dying in the service of the poor, in the arms of providence, and with genuine renouncement of ourselves in order to follow Jesus Christ.[2]

Saint Vincent offers no systematic philosophical or theological analysis of providence. But the documents we possess, particularly his letters written to fit particular occasions and to respond to individuals whose

---

1. Article originally published in *Vincentiana* 6 (Rome: Curia Generalitia, 1993) 594-614.
2. SV III, 392 (letter to Jean Barreau, French consul in Algiers).

personalities were quite varied, give us considerable insight into how he understood it. In differing circumstances, providence takes on different shades of meaning for him.

God's hidden plan works for good

We owe some of Saint Vincent's most striking statements on providence to Louise de Marillac. As she struggled, particularly in the upbringing of her son Michel, she disclosed her pain to Saint Vincent. He encouraged her to do her best, to be at peace, and to place the rest in God's hands.

He writes to her in 1629: "I wish you good evening and hope that you are no longer weeping over the happiness of your little Michel . . . . *Mon Dieu*, my daughter, what great hidden treasures there are in holy providence and how marvelously our Lord is honored by those who follow it and do not try to get ahead of it!" (SV I, 68).

He tells Saint Louise in 1634, in a delicate situation involving the Bishop of Beauvais: "Follow the order of providence. Oh! how good it is to let ourselves be guided by it!" (SV I, 241).

He was convinced that, when he had to go away on business, God himself in his providence would provide spiritual direction for Saint Louise, and he assured her of this (cf. SV I, 26).

The need to follow providence comes up again and again as Saint Vincent writes to various confreres during his lengthy negotiations in Rome. In 1640 he tells Louis Lebreton, who was encountering obstacles in trying to get a house for the Congregation: "I know that nothing can be added to your diligence and that this [bad situation] is not due to you personally, to your zeal, nor your handling of the matter. Our Lord has given you both and is directing this matter according to the order of his eternal providence. Be assured, Monsieur, that you will see in this situation that it is for the best, and I think I can already see it as clearly as the light of day. O Monsieur, how good it is to let oneself be guided by his providence!" (SV II, 137).

Vincent is utterly convinced that for those who love God and seek to do his will, "all things work together for good" (Rom 8:28). "In the name of God, let us not be surprised at anything. God will do everything for the best," he tells Louise de Marillac in 1647 (SV III, 213). He tells Achille le Vazeux: "Let us place ourselves in complete dependence on God, with confidence that, in doing that, everything which people say or do against us will work out for the good" (SV IV, 393). Just before his death he writes to René Alméras: "God be praised, Monsieur, for all that he allows to happen to us! Certainly I would have great difficulty bearing these things if I did not regard them as God's good pleasure, which orders everything for good" (SV VIII, 376).

"The Lord does not allow anything to happen without a reason. We do not know it at present, but one day we will see it," he writes to Jean Barreau, in 1658. In the same year he tells Edme Jolly, the superior in Rome, "His providence alone is what takes care of this sort of affair. . . . The usage of the Company has always been to await and not to run ahead of the higher order" (SV VII, 385-86).[3]

Saint Vincent appeals to God's hidden plan in many varied circumstances: to explain the surprising success of the works he had started (SV XII, 7), to console the Company when speaking of the sickness or death of missionaries (SV XI, 47; XI, 100), to make sense out of the loss of the Orsigny farm (SV XII, 53), to encourage those who lost their parents (SV VI, 444), to find meaning in the sudden departure of Missionaries or Daughters of Charity from the Company (SV IX, 481-82), to urge the Company to accept calumny and persecution with courage (CR II, 13).

He is so convinced of the importance of following providence for the Daughters of Charity that he even imagines their being called Daughters of Providence: "O my Daughters, you should have such great devotion to, such great confidence and love in, divine providence, that if providence itself had not given you the beautiful name of Daughters of Charity, you should bear that of Daughters of Providence, for it was providence that brought you into being" (SV IX, 74).[4]

Peacefully and patiently waiting for God's plan

This theme comes through very strongly in Saint Vincent's letters to the impetuous Bernard Codoing, the superior in Rome, who often aroused the founder's ire by moving too quickly or too brusquely. After rebuking Codoing rather sharply in a letter written on December 7, 1641, and after telling him to act with greater deliberation, Saint Vincent adds: "Reflect-

---

3. Cf. also SV V, 164; X, 506.
4. Cf. also SV IX, 113-114; IX, 243-46.

ing on all the principal events that have taken place in this Company, it seems to me, and this is quite evident, that, if they had taken place before they did, they would not have been successful. I say that of all of them, without excepting a single one. That is why I have a particular devotion to following the adorable providence of God step by step. And my only consolation is that I think our Lord alone has carried on and is constantly carrying on the business of the Little Company" (SV II, 208). On March 16, 1644, Vincent reprimands Codoing for interfering in matters that are not his concern: "In the name of God, Monsieur, stop being concerned about things happening far away that are none of your business, and devote all your attention to domestic discipline. The rest will come in due time. Grace has its moments. Let us abandon ourselves to the providence of God and be on our guard against anticipating it. If our Lord is pleased to give me any consolation in our vocation it is this: I think, it seems to me, that we have tried to follow divine providence in all things and to put our feet only in the place it has marked out for us" (SV II, 453).

In another letter to Codoing later in 1644 he states: "'The consolation that our Lord gives me is to think that, by the grace of God, we have always tried to follow and not run ahead of providence, which knows so wisely how to lead everything to the goal that our Lord destines for it" (SV II, 456). Three months later he adds: "But what are we going to do, you say? We will do what our Lord wills, which is to keep ourselves always in dependence on his providence" (SV II, 469).

He summarizes the point for Codoing on August 6, 1644: "I have told you on previous occasions, Monsieur, that the things of God come about by themselves, and that wisdom consists in following providence step by step. And you can be sure of the truth of a maxim which seems paradoxical, namely that he who is hasty falls back in the interests of God" (SV II, 472-73).

There is a clear tension in Saint Vincent's writings between activity and passivity. His attitude depended greatly on the circumstances. For instance, in trying to moderate the indiscreet zeal of Philippe le Vacher, he urges passivity: "The good that God wishes to be done comes about almost by itself, without our thinking about it. That is the way the Congregation was born, that the missions and the retreats to ordinands began, that the Company of the Daughters of Charity came into being. . . . *Mon Dieu!* Monsieur, how I desire that you would moderate your ardor and weigh things maturely on the scale of the sanctuary before resolving them! Be passive rather than active. In that way God will do through you alone what the whole world together could not do without him" (SV IV, 122-23). He often emphasizes this theme to Louise de Marillac: "All things come to the one who waits. This is true, as a rule, even more in the things of God than in others" (SV I, 233).[5]

In all this, it is quite evident that Saint Vincent abhorred rushing. He tells others that "God's spirit is neither violent nor hasty" (SV II, 226), "his works have their moment" (SV II, 453), they are done "almost by themselves" (SV II, 473, 466; IV, 122), they are accomplished "little by little" (SV VII, 216; II, 226). "In the name of God, Monsieur," he tells Codoing, "if necessity urges us to make haste, then let it be slowly, as the wise proverb says" (SV II, 276).

But, as is suggested in the citation above, there is another side to this truth to be found in Saint Vincent's teaching.

God's co-workers must make haste, even if slowly

Saint Vincent takes the opposite side of the same passivity/activity theme with Étienne Blatiron, the superior in Rome in 1655. The emphasis shifts subtly as Saint Vincent makes it clear that he is eager for some action: "Do not stop pursuing our business, with confidence that it is God's good pleasure. . . . Success in matters like this is often due to the patience and vigilance that one exercises. . . . The works of God have their moment. His providence does them then, and not sooner or later. . . . Let us wait patiently, but let us act, and, so to speak, let us make haste slowly in negotiating one of the most important affairs that the Congregation will ever have" (SV V, 396).

The tension between activity and passivity within Saint Vincent himself is evident in another letter he writes to Étienne Blatiron on November 12, 1655. In it he comments favorably on a practice that Blatiron had begun, namely to ask, through the intercession of Saint Joseph, for the spreading of the Company. He adds reflectively: "For twenty years I have not dared to ask that of God, thinking that, since the Congregation is his

---

5. In a similar vein, but in very different circumstances, in 1659 he tells Jacques Pesnelles, who was initiating one-day retreats for the local community: "Since God does not depend on time, he sometimes works more graces in one day than in eight" (SV VIII, 70).

work, we should leave to his providence alone the responsibility for its conservation and its growth. But, struck by the recommendation made to us in the gospel, to ask him to send laborers into the harvest, I have become convinced of the importance and usefulness of this devotion" (SV V, 463).[6]

Finally, if anyone should be tempted to interpret Saint Vincent's teaching on providence too passively, he might recall the founder's words to Edme Jolly: "You are one of the few men who honor the providence of God very much by the preparation of remedies against foreseen evils. I thank you very humbly for this and pray that our Lord will continue to enlighten you more and more so that such enlightenment may spread through the Company" (SV VII, 310).

Following providence and doing the will of God in all things

One of the early, abiding influences on Saint Vincent's thought is Benedict of Canfield's *Rule of Perfection*, in which doing the will of God in all things is described as the central element in the spiritual life.[7]

From many of the citations above, the reader has already noted how central doing the will of God is for Saint Vincent. In the period of Louise de Marillac's anguish over her son Michel's future, he writes to her about another problem concerning a small infant, and then adds: "In any case, God will provide for the child and for your son as well, without your giving way to anxiety about what will become of him. Give the child and the mother to our Lord. He will take good care of you and your son. Just let him do his will in you and in him, and await it in all your exercises. All you need to do is to devote yourself entirely to God. Oh! how little it takes to be very holy: to do the will of God in all things" (SV II, 36).

The close link between doing the will of God and following providence

---

6. But cf. SV VI, 177; VIII, 287.
7. Benedict of Canfield, an English Capuchin named William Fitch (1562-1611), having been converted from Puritanism, took refuge in France. He had enormous influence on his contemporaries and was a much sought-after spiritual director. Bremond states that his *Rule of Perfection* was the manual for two or three generations of mystics, calling him "the master of masters." Cf. *Histoire littéraire du sentiment religieux en France* (Paris, 1916 and 1928), II:155-58, as well as VII:266. Cf. also T. Davitt, "An Introduction to Benet of Canfield," *Colloque* 16 (1987) 268-82. Dodin points out that Saint Vincent read Canfield's *Rule of Perfection* in the 1609 edition, which was considerably different from subsequent ones, and that he was inspired by it throughout his life, sometimes copying it even literally, as in SV I, 68-69.

is a recurrent theme in Saint Vincent's letters. He writes to René Alméras on May 10, 1647: "O Monsieur, what a happiness to will nothing but what God wills, to do nothing but what is in accord with the occasion providence presents, and to have nothing but what God in his providence has given us!" (SV III, 188).

The clearest influence of Canfield's doctrine on Saint Vincent is evident in the conference of March 7, 1659, where he describes the process of discerning and doing God's will (SV XII, 150-165).

We must "will what divine providence wills" (SV VI, 476) is one of the ways Saint Vincent puts it, combining the two themes. He tells the Missionaries: "Perfection consists in so uniting our will to God's that his will and ours, properly speaking, form only one will and non-will" (SV XI, 318).

The two foundations of Saint Vincent's teaching on providence[8]

1) Confidence in God

Trust in providence is the ability to place oneself in the hands of God as a loving Father.

"Let us give ourselves to God," Saint Vincent says repeatedly to the Vincentians, as well as to the Daughters of Charity.[9] He has deep confidence in God as his Father, into whose hands he can place himself and his works. The journal written by Jean Gicquel recounts how Vincent told Frs. Alméras, Berthe, and Gicquel, on June 7, 1660, just four months before his death: "To be consumed for God, to have no goods nor power except for the purpose of consuming them for God—that is what our Savior did himself, who was consumed for love of his Father" (SV XIII, 179).

Saint Vincent wanted love for God to be all-embracing. He writes to Pierre Escart: "I greatly hope we may set about stripping ourselves entirely of affection for anything that is not God, be attached to things only for God and according to God, and that we may seek and establish

---

8. Cf. SV V, 403.
9. Cf. SV I, 253; III, 221, 291, 403; V, 195, 233, 320, 425, 440, 484, 626; VI, 68; VII, 613; VIII, 463; XI 26, 157; XII, 166, 221, 291, 403. For a striking statement of Saint Vincent's attitude before God, cf. SV XII, 133-134, 146-147.

his kingdom first of all in ourselves, and then in others. That is what I entreat you to ask of him for me" (SV II, 106).

Saint Vincent is profoundly convinced that, because God loves us deeply as a Father, he exercises a continual providence in our lives. He writes to Achille le Vazeux: "[God] knows what is suitable for us, and if, like good children, we abandon ourselves to so good a Father, he will give it to us at the proper moment" (SV VI, 308).

Many of Vincent's conferences and writings speak of the providence of *God* (implicitly, and sometimes explicitly, the Father);[10] many others speak of *Christ's* providence for his followers.[11]

He tells the Daughters: "To have confidence in providence means that we should hope that God takes care of those who serve him, as a husband takes care of his wife or a father of his child. That is how—and far more truly—God takes care of us. We have only to abandon ourselves to his guidance, as the Rule says, just as 'a little child does to its nurse.' If she puts it on her right arm, the child is quite content; if she moves him over to her left, he doesn't care, he is quite satisfied provided he has her breast. We should, then, have the same confidence in divine providence, seeing that it takes care of all that concerns us, just as a nursing mother takes care of her baby" (SV X, 503).

Speaking of the providence which Jesus himself has for his followers, Saint Vincent tells Jean Martin in 1647: "So, Father, let us ask our Lord that everything might be done in accordance with his providence, that our wills be submitted to him in such a way that between him and us there might be only one, which will enable us to enjoy his unique love in time and in eternity" (SV III, 197). One notes here again the strong influence of Benedict of Canfield on Saint Vincent.

2) Indifference

Saint Vincent speaks at length on this subject in his conference to the Missionaries on May 16, 1659 (SV XII, 227-44). Here too the influence of Canfield is evident.

Indifference, for Saint Vincent, is detachment from all things that would keep us from God (SV XII, 228). It sets us free to be united with

---

10. Cf. SV II, 473; III, 188; V, 396; VIII, 152.
11. This may not always be an intentional distinction since in Vincent's writings sometimes the actions of the Father are not clearly distinguished from those of the Son.

him (SV XII, 229-30), disposing us to will only what he wills (cf. CR II, 10). It is indispensably linked with trust in providence. "Our Lord is a continual Communion for those who are united to what he wills and does not will," he tells Louise de Marillac (SV I, 233). He repeats this advice to her again and again: "It is necessary to accept God's way of acting toward your Daughters, to offer them to him, and to remain in peace. The Son of God saw his company dispersed and almost wiped out forever. You must unite your will with his" (SV V, 420).

To a priest of the Mission he writes: "What shall we do in that regard but will what providence wills, and not will what it does not will?" (SV VI, 476).

He speaks lyrically to the Daughters of Charity on the theme: "To do the will of God is to begin paradise in this world. Give me a Daughter who does for her whole life the will of God. She begins to do on earth what the blessed do in heaven. She begins her paradise even in this world" (SV IX, 645).

Some Horizon-Shifts between the Seventeenth and Twentieth Centuries

The problematic which I have described in the previous chapter on the cross applies to providence as well; I will not, therefore, repeat it here. A theology of the cross and a theology of providence are closely intertwined. This is evident in the writings of Saint Vincent and Saint Louise, where the two themes often occur in the same context.[12]

Keeping in mind what has already been stated about the cross, here I will mention only briefly two other factors that influence the way one views providence; namely, two horizon-shifts that have taken place between Saint Vincent's time and ours.

1. From an era of direct causality to one of secondary causes and autonomy of the human person

This shift was already taking place in Saint Vincent's time. Today it is very much a part of the air we breathe. In a scientific era, one focuses

---

12. Cf., for example, Saint Louise's words to Jeanne Lepintre: "It is perhaps for that reason, my dear Sister, that our Lord inspires you to remain at peace at the foot of his cross, completely submissive to the guidance of his divine providence" (SW 416).

on empirical data. Both well-being and disease are attributed to discernible causes, rather than directly to God. Even when the cause of a disease is unknown, we search for it today with the conviction that it will eventually be found. In that context, attributing good or evil to God's providence can sometimes sound quaint, or occasionally, hollow. Even worse, when someone is confronted with serious problems, the exhortation to abandon oneself to providence may run contrary to prudence, which instead urges us to seek remedies for our ills. Of course, this shift in emphasis is not entirely new. Catholic moral theology has, in fact, consistently placed strong emphasis on the role of secondary causes, since it has always placed great emphasis on human responsibility. Moreover, Catholic systematic theology, with its stress on mediation, has often similarly accented secondary causes.[13]

Particularly since *Gaudium et Spes* (cf. #s 4, 9, 12, 14, 15, 22), Catholic theology has emphasized the autonomy of the human person. One is surely slower today than in Saint Vincent's time to attribute things directly to God when they are more evidently of human doing.

We are conscious too that this way of thinking lets "God be God," so to speak. It recognizes his ultimate autonomy, his complete otherness. It recognizes too that his causality does not diminish human freedom, but is the ground for it; in fact, dependence on God and genuine human autonomy increase, rather than decrease, in direct proportion to one another.[14] God's power does not enslave human beings; it empowers them.[15]

In this same perspective, the human person is seen as being in process, as incomplete but open to the absolute. Change is accepted not only as inevitable, but as desirable. Rapid change, moreover, has become part of life, and its rate seems to be growing exponentially. In this age of computers, we are convinced that we can "make things happen" and that we can eventually find the solution to almost all problems that arise.

---

13. C. Curran, "Providence and Responsibility: the Divine and the Human in History from the Perspective of Moral Theology," in *Proceedings of the Forty-Fourth Annual Convention of the Catholic Theological Society of America* XLIV (Louisville, 1989) 44-45.
14. Cf. K. Rahner, *Theological Investigations* V (Baltimore: Helicon, 1966) 166.
15. Cf. *Gaudium et Spes*, 34.

2. *A shift from a static to a historical way of viewing the world*

The ways in which we view the world, the human person, and God are intimately intertwined and affect our view of providence as well. Different ways of viewing these realities characterize different epochs but sometimes also exist simultaneously within the same epoch. Here, let me briefly decribe three.[16]

In a *static* understanding, such as prevailed in the fifteenth and sixteenth centuries, and into Saint Vincent's time, the view of the human person is a-historical. Society has established orders, which are accepted as divinely willed. External laws and rules prevail. The political, economic and social spheres are governed by the established laws. Within this context the emphasis in one's view of God is on the Absolute, the All-Powerful, the Omnipresent, the Omniscient. In speaking of providence, one sees God as ruling over all and directing all. Faith in providence takes the form of abandonment and absolute confidence in God's plan which never fails. As is evident, this perspective has brought rich benefits to the lives of many saints, including Vincent de Paul and Louise de Marillac, but there is a danger, for some, that this understanding of God's providence can lead to escapism or lack of responsibility.

In a *personalist* understanding of reality, which has emerged increasingly since the eighteenth century, as the "rights of man" have come to be emphasized, the autonomy and liberty of the human person come to the fore. Human responsibility and creativity are accented. In ethics the emphasis lies on interiorization and conscience. In theology, history and process are highlighted. The Church is seen as the body of Christ. In speaking of God one emphasizes his personal love as Father. In talking about providence, one sees God as guiding each of us in his or her personal history. God loves us; he walks with us and leads us. While there are many advantages to this perspective, particularly on the level of conviction about God's love and the need for personal conversion, there is a danger that this understanding of God and providence can fall into "intimism."[17]

In a *historical-social* understanding of reality the emphasis is on the

---

16. Cf. Lúcia Weiler, "A Divina Providência passa pela organizaçâo e a partilha humana," *Convergência*, vol. XXVIII, n. 259 (January 1993) 21-37.

17. *Intimism* is used here to describe a type of piety that focuses sharply on one's personal relationship with God but fails to give sufficient attention to the social and societal dimensions of that relationship.

inter-relationship of people within a societal context and the building up of the human family. In ethics social responsibility is highlighted. The transformation of society and socio-political reality is underlined. Sin too is understood in a social context.[18] There is a call to change unjust social structures. In theology the Trinitarian God is emphasized. The Church is viewed as the people of God, living in a permanent exodus. When one speaks of providence, one speaks of God as the liberator of his people, freeing them from the bonds of oppression. This perspective has the advantage of moving toward concrete and fundamental resolution of social problems, which keep the poor poor; for some, it bears the risk of falling into an activism that loses focus on God's ways.

Re-visiting Providence Today

There is much re-examination of providence today,[19] with a view toward articulating a theology that, while recognizing various levels of causality, accounts for both the rational and irrational within human existence and can find meaning where we experience chaos, disorder, violence and apathy. A theology of providence is at its root a theology of *meaning*. It seeks to bridge the gap between the polarities of human experience: design and chaos, health and sickness, life and death, grace and sin, care and non-care, plan and disruption, peace and violence. Ministers of providence are those men and women whose lives witness to meaning and who can speak meaning. Docility to providence is an attitude of reverent trust before the mystery of God, as revealed in Christ, in whom life, death, and resurrection are integrated.[20]

Trust in providence means rootedness in a loving, personal God

Belief in providence shows itself throughout history not so much in credal statements as in the trusting words of daily prayer. It is inseparable from faith in a loving, personal God.

---

18. Cf. *Puebla*, 28.
19. Cf. the entire issue of the *Proceedings of the Forty-Fourth Annual Convention of the Catholic Theological Society of America* XLIV.
20. Cf. Barbara Doherty, "Providence and Histories: Some American Views," *Proceedings of the Forty-Fourth Annual Convention of the Catholic Theological Society of America* XLIV, 2-3.

The human mind balks at mystery. Yet we encounter it again and again at the base of our deepest joys and our deepest sorrows. Birth, death, beauty, tragedy—all are shrouded in mystery. We continually struggle to reconcile opposites, to plumb the depths of life and death. As early as the fifth century B.C., the Greeks, particularly the stoics, use the term *providence* to denote a rational order of things where a divine reason pervades everything. This term enters the Old Testament rather late in the books of Job and Wisdom, where it joins an earlier strain that focuses not so much on a philosophical concept of cosmic harmony, but on God as acting in history. This fundamental Old Testament belief sees God as allied with his people. He is active in creating, covenanting, chastising, forgiving, liberating. He is with his people both in their conquests and in their captivity. He goes with them into exile and he returns with them. "Can a mother forget her infant, be without tenderness for the child of her womb? Even should she forget, I will never forget you. See, upon the palms of my hands I have written your name" (Is 49:15-16).

This provident God of the Hebrew scriptures is the God of Jesus Christ. He is the Father whom Jesus loves and who captures his entire attention. Jesus' death and resurrection are the ultimate proclamation of providence.

At the heart of New Testament faith is belief in a personal God, who reveals himself as Father in his Son Jesus, who takes on human flesh. Jesus himself struggles with the mysteries of life, growth, success, desertion by his followers, pain, and death. He finds the resolution of the struggle, not in some clearly stated philosophy that he outlines for future ages, but in commending himself into the hands of his Father. He trusts that his Father loves him deeply and that he can bring joy from sorrow, life from death.

The New Testament, reflecting on Jesus' experience, tells us again and again to focus on the personal love of God for us. Jesus extols, in a passage that Saint Vincent loved (cf. SV XII, 142), God's providence for his children: "Consider the lilies of the field. They do not work; they do not spin. Yet I assure you, not even Solomon in all his splendor was arrayed like one of these. If God can clothe in such splendor the grass of the field, which blooms today and is thrown on the fire tomorrow, will he not provide much more for you, O weak in faith" (Mt 6:28-30; cf. Lk 12:27).

Luke's writings highlight God's providence in a special way.[21] The

---

21. Cf. J. Schultz, "Gottes Vorsehung bei Lukas," *Zeitschrift für die neutestamentiche Wissenschaft* 54 (1963), 104-16.

Spirit of the Father and of Jesus is active from the beginning in Luke, guiding the course of history. He anoints Jesus with power from on high and directs him and his disciples in their ministry.[22]

> * The Holy Spirit will come down on you and the power of the Most High will overshadow you (Lk 1:35).

> * Having received baptism . . . the Holy Spirit descended on him (Lk 3:22).

> * Jesus, filled with the Holy Spirit . . . was led by the Spirit into the desert (Lk 4:1).

> * Jesus returned to Galilee with the power of the Holy Spirit (Lk 4:14).

> * The Spirit of the Lord is upon me (Lk 4:18).

> * Your heavenly Father will give the Holy Spirit to those who ask him (Lk 11:13).

> * The Holy Spirit will teach you at that moment what you should say (Lk 12:12).

One of the crucial signs of faith in a personal God is confident prayer. The very act of praying states that we believe that God is alive, that he relates to us, that he listens, that he cares about our journey, that he hears the cries of the poor especially, and that he responds. It is for this reason that Luke's gospel insists so frequently on trusting, persistent prayer (cf. Lk 11:1-13; 18:1-8).

Hoping in God's wisdom and power

Trust in providence implies trust in an unseen wisdom that guides the events of history and that is able to reconcile opposites.

We sometimes get glimpses of a larger picture where tragedy works for good. Destructive floods provide fertile land for the future. Enormous fires ravage forests, doing huge damage, but purifying them for luxuriant growth in the future. Pain and suffering at times mature a person and help him or her to grow in compassion and understanding for others.

---

22. The Book of the Acts of the Apostles continues this theme of the "Gospel of the Holy Spirit." There are fifty-seven references to the Spirit in Acts; cf. J. Fitzmyer, *The Gospel According to Luke*, in *Anchor Bible*, vol. 28, 227.

In a striking Greek myth, the infant Demophoön is placed in the care of the divine mother Demeter, who caresses him, nurses him, breathes on him, and anoints him with ambrosia. At night she places him in a fire to make him immortal. When his mother discovers this, she cries out in fear. But Demeter responds: "You don't know when fate is bringing you something good or something bad!" Demeter is giving a lesson in nursing. She shows that motherhood involves nurturing not only in human ways but also in divine ways. Holding the child in the fire is a way of burning away those elements that resist immortality.[23]

The "hidden plan" of God is a theme that Saint Paul returns to frequently. It is revealed in Christ, who brings together death and life, but its fullness is revealed only in the end-time when all things are subjected to Christ (Eph 1:9) and through him to the Father (1 Cor 15:28). "God has given us the wisdom to understand fully the mystery, the plan he was pleased to decree in Christ, to be carried out in the fullness of time: namely, to bring all things in the heavens and on earth into one under Christ's headship" (Eph 1:9-10). The Pauline letters speak of "the mystery of Christ in you, your hope of glory" (Col 1:27), "the mystery of God—namely Christ—in whom every treasure of wisdom and knowledge is hidden" (Col 2:2-3).

But, as the texts themselves state, God's wisdom remains a mystery, "a stumbling block to the Jews and foolishness to the gentiles" (1 Cor 1:23). The mystery of the cross and resurrection of Jesus, the center of Christian hope and the symbol of God's providence, provides no explanation of the reconciliation of opposites. It calls us, rather, to say with Jesus: "Father, into your hands I commend my spirit" (Lk 23:46). The cross proclaims that the power of God overcomes human weakness, bringing life from death, and that the wisdom of God surpasses the limits of human reasoning, bringing light to the darkness.

Prudence, patience, and perseverance

It is striking how often Saint Vincent emphasizes good timing. He is utterly convinced that grace has its moments. Some of the classical works of literature contemporary with Saint Vincent witness to the same truth in more secular language. "There is special providence in the fall of a

---

23. Cf. Thomas Moore, *Care of the Soul* (New York: Harper Collins, 1992) 44.

sparrow. If it be now, 'tis not to come; if it be not to come, it will be now; if it be not now, yet it will come. The readiness is all," states Hamlet.[24] In a more violent context, Brutus states in *Julius Caesar:* "There is a tide in the affairs of men, which, taken at the flood, leads on to fortune. Omitted, all the voyage of their life is bound in shallows and miseries. On such a full sea are we now afloat, and we must take the current when it serves, or lose our ventures" (IV. iii. 217-23).

When used to describe a good sense of timing, docility to providence involves patient waiting, not in a passive sense, but with an active capacity for knowing the right moment to act. From this perspective, it is synonymous with prudence, patience, and perseverance. Sometimes the right moment comes quickly; at other times, it arrives slowly. Sometimes it arrives unexpectedly, with almost no preparation; at other times, it reveals itself only with considerable prodding.

Often only the persevering see the fruit of patient waiting. A good example of this was the successful, but painfully slow, series of negotiations concerning the vows of the Congregation, which Saint Vincent guided to their conclusion. The process took two decades to complete. Some of Saint Vincent's most eloquent statements about the need to follow providence come from those years. But he also reminded his representatives in the negotiations that providence is honored by using the means that God places at our disposal for accomplishing his goals.[25]

We are active sharers in God's providence

Aquinas pointed out long ago that providence acts upon us not just as *objects*, but acts in and through us also as *subjects*: "The rational creature is subject to divine providence in a most excellent way, insofar as it partakes of a share of providence, by being provident both for itself and for others."[26] God acts not only upon, but in and through, free human beings. His freedom does not diminish but creates and enhances ours. His providence, then, works not only through the events of nature, through sickness and health, through life and death, through history, but through *us* personally. Not only God is responsible for the world, but we are too.

---

24. *Hamlet* V. ii. 229; cf. *King Lear* V. ii. 10-12: "Ripeness is all."
25. SV V, 396: "Let us wait patiently, but let us act, and, as it were, let us make haste slowly."
26. *Summa Theologica* II/I, 91, 2.

Each human person, therefore, bears responsibility in relationship to himself, to other persons, to groups within society, to the political order, to the natural resources around us. "Action on behalf of justice and participation in the transformation of the world" is one of the fundamental responsibilities of the Church and all its members today.[27]

Let me suggest four precisions about this responsibility:

a. Each person shares in it. All are called to work toward a more just social order. This demands foresight (*providere* = "to see beforehand") and action. The truly provident person can play a prophetic role within the human community by naming the ways of justice, even before society is ready to walk in them, and by calling for conversion to those ways. Charting the future and wise planning are a part of providence.

b. The responsibility of each person is limited. Some can do more, some less. In order to concretize one's personal contribution (and to avoid being overwhelmed by guilt or by the vastness of the world's problems), it may be well to select a single area where we can genuinely focus our energies and leave other areas to other persons. We are not alone in bearing responsibility.

c. An individual's responsibility fits, moreover, within the larger context of his or her other duties (such as taking care of one's own family, doing one's job, etc.), within which it must be weighed.

d. No matter how active one might be, there will always be much that must be left in the hands of God. There will be times when nothing can be done. There will be inevitable sickness and death. There will be moments of powerlessness before the violence of others or the misused freedom of others.

In this era when the Church makes a preferential option for the poor, one must ask the question: How will God's providence be shown toward them? It will be shown particularly when *we* provide for the needs of the poor. God's providence for them in their needs really becomes evident in a tangible way only when God's people are active in solidarity with the poor.

Saint Vincent was quite aware that trust in God's providence did not absolve him from his own responsibility to act. He was, in fact, very active, even while affirming that God was doing everything. Contempo-

---

27. Synod of Bishops, 1971, *Justice in the World*, in *Acta Apostolicae Sedis* LXIII (1971) 924; henceforth, *AAS*.

rary theology emphasizes that God's action will often coincide with our action, as is quite evident in Saint Vincent's life and works.

Saint Vincent was also very aware, however, of the need for prudence and for a good sense of timing. Some are inclined to act too hastily, plucking the fruit from the tree before it is ripe. Others are inclined to wait too long, leaving the fruit on the tree until it falls and rots. Grace has its moments, Saint Vincent said. It is important to know when the right moment has arrived.

Our own providence takes nothing away from God's providence. Rather, it manifests it. Even when we are very active, we can still thank God for the gifts that he works in and through us. "He who is mighty has done great things to me and holy is his name" (Lk 1:49). Providence today, therefore, can take the form of active concern for

Oneself	One's Health, One's On-going Formation
Other Persons	Attentiveness To The Needs Of The Poor
Societal Groups	Socio-political Involvement
The Poor	Action On Behalf Of Justice, Charity
Nature	Care Of The Environment

A Parable

I offer this parable, which I have freely adapted from several ancient stories, for all those who struggle to believe in providence.

Once upon a time in a far distant land, there lived a young man named Pilgrim. Filled with energy from birth, he seemed to leap from his mother's womb.

One day, when the years of playing games and swinging from trees had come to an end, he set out in search of life's meaning.

At that time, in a remote mountain village dwelt a man renowned for holiness. Pilgrim journeyed to the saint's tiny abode and found him in deep prayer. "What must I do," Pilgrim asked, "to live life to the full?"

The saint gave him a Bible and a sleeping mat and led him into the mountains until they came to a tiny cave by the side of a river. "Stay here, till I return," the saint said, "and God will provide everything." Then he left him.

Pilgrim found the autumn days long and lonely at first. Seated by the river he read his Bible and meditated on its words. He ate the abundant fish he caught and drank pure water from the stream. In the cold of the winter he stayed mostly in the cave, reading and praying by the fire. In the spring he transferred to a rock by the river where he saw the trees bud and the flowers bloom. He even slept there in the summer, the hardness of the rock being softened by the sound of the water's flow.

With the passing of a second year a deep peace welled up in Pilgrim's heart, but he did wonder why the saint delayed so long in returning.

Ten years went by, with the earth's rhythms of light and darkness, warmth and cold, blooming and withering. Pilgrim's body grew strong and hard; his spirit was tranquil.

One day the saint returned. Pilgrim baked a large fish, which they ate by the river, drinking from its plentiful waters. He noted that the saint now seemed much older. "Do you really think that there is life after death?" Pilgrim asked him. "The prior question," the saint replied, "is: is there really life before death?" That evening the saint led him back to the village and placed him at the head of a household with seven orphaned children. "Provide for them until I return," the saint said and left him.

The orphans ranged in age from seven to twelve, so Pilgrim set out to be a father and a mother to them. He made many mistakes at first since he knew little about parenting, but slowly the children began to love him, and he them. He prepared their meals, taught them to read and write, and advised them in the joys and pains of growing up.

As the years went on, the children matured well. Pilgrim found himself very happy. His reputation grew in the village and the people began to regard him as a holy man.

Soon many came from east and west to speak with Pilgrim and to consult him about their lives. His gentleness and wisdom became renowned in the land. His family of orphans had grown up by now and had learned to take care of themselves, so Pilgrim devoted more and more time to those who sought him. Eventually, so many came that he had no time for anything else. Though he was tired, he sensed fulfillment within himself. His children urged him to rest more, to read and to cultivate the land as he had once done, but a drive to bear the burdens of others gnawed away within him.

One night a young woman came to seek his counsel. It happened to be his birthday, so his orphan children had brought him a feast of baked fish from the stream and rich new wine from the grapes just harvested in the mountains. They had eaten and drunk in abundance. The crowds visiting Pilgrim that day were great, so he could speak with the young woman only after the feast. A new passion stirred within him that night and, overcome with weariness and wine, he slept with her.

When Pilgrim awoke late the next morning, his family and the whole village knew. Filled with shame, he fled to his cave in the mountains. There he wept.

Another life began for Pilgrim that day. He gave himself to penance and to reading his Bible again and meditating on its words. He ate a single meal in the evening and slept on the hard ground of his cave. He cultivated a small field along the river bank and twice a year sent its harvest to the poor of the village, with a message to his orphaned children that he loved them.

After Pilgrim had lived thus for seven years, the saint returned to visit him again. He was very old now. As they sat at the fire that evening, eating a fish caught in the stream, Pilgrim asked the saint: "Have you finished your work here on earth?" "I have half finished," the saint answered. "I have proclaimed justice for the poor and liberty for the oppressed. The needy have listened eagerly, but I am not so sure that the well-off have heard my words."

The next morning the saint led Pilgrim to the village again. That year a terrible drought had brought famine upon the land.

"Provide food for the people," the saint said, "and stay here till I return." Pilgrim was perplexed at first, but he remembered that water flowed abundantly in the river near his cave in the mountains, so he led half the men and women of the village to go there to plant and harvest. They slept on the hard ground, rising each morning to praise God for his gifts and working till evening, when they baked and ate the fish they caught in the river.

The village lay five miles downhill from the river. The other half of its men and women worked there under Pilgrim's oldest orphan son. They dug troughs over the sloping land until, a year later, water ran down into the village fields. That day Pilgrim led all the people in prayer, rejoicing in the gifts that God had given them.

From that time on, the crops sprouted regularly in the fields and the poor ate abundantly. And the renown of Pilgrim's holiness grew greater than it had ever been before.

On the evening when the waters ran downhill, the saint came to visit Pilgrim a final time. He died in his house that night. His last words to Pilgrim were these: "Trust deeply in God, and the sun will shine on you even in the night."

Pilgrim knew that God provides and that the saint had directed him well.

The Maternal Face of Jesus
A Note on Vincent de Paul[1]

There is much that one could say about Vincent de Paul's relationship with women. Among his closest friends and collaborators were two women saints, Jane Frances de Chantal and Louise de Marillac. Other women played a very significant role in his life, and he in theirs: from the unlettered peasant girl, Marguerite Naseau, to the Queen of France, Anne of Austria.

Some have even suggested tentatively that, in his role as a leader, Saint Vincent related better to, and had a more significant influence on, women than men.[2] While that judgment may be difficult to sustain, given Saint Vincent's formidable array of male friends and counselees, he surely did have an impressive list of female admirers and collaborators: Madame de Gondi, Jane Frances de Chantal, Louise de Marillac, Madame Goussault, Mademoiselle du Fay, Anne of Austria, Marie de Gonzague—just to name a few.

It would be a mistake to think that his relationship with these women was "purely business." He related to them with warmth and affection, without, as he might put it, "the slightest suspicion of unchastity" (CR IV, 1).

His letters contain some lovely passages filled with human warmth. In October 1627 he tells Louise de Marillac: "I am writing to you at about midnight and am a little tired. Forgive my heart if it is not a little more expansive in this letter. Be faithful to your faithful lover who is our Lord. Also be very simple and humble. And I shall be in the love of our Lord and his holy mother . . . " (SV I, 30). On New Year's Day 1638, he concludes his letter to her: "I wish you a young heart and a love in its first bloom for him who loves us unceasingly and as tenderly as if He were just beginning to love us. For all God's pleasures are ever new and full

---

1. Article originally published in *Vincentiana* 3 (Rome: Curia Generalitia, 1994) 144-48 and *Colloque* 29 (Spring 1994) 355-61.
2. Cf. Jaime Corera, "St. Vincent and Human Formation," *Vincentian Heritage* 9 (#1; 1988) 79.

of variety, although he never changes. I am in his love, with an affection such as his goodness desires and which I owe him out of love for him, Mademoiselle, your most humble servant . . . " (SV I, 417-18).

To Jane Frances de Chantal, he writes: "And now, my dear Mother, permit me to ask if your incomparable kindness still allows me the happiness of enjoying the place you have given me in your dear and most amiable heart? I certainly hope so, although my miseries make me unworthy of it" (SV I, 566). In another letter to her, he describes Saint Jane Frances as someone who is "so much our honored Mother that she is mine alone, and whom I honor and cherish more tenderly than any child ever honored and loved its mother since our Lord; and it seems to me that I do so to such an extent that I have sufficient esteem and love to be able to share it with the whole world; and that, in truth, without exaggeration" (SV II, 86-87).

From his writings, it is evident that Vincent's esteem for women was very high. He was inclined to think, for instance, that women are apt to be better administrators than men (cf. SV IV, 71). He had no doubts that God wanted them to have an equal role in the service of the poor. In his famous conference on "The End of the Congregation of the Mission," given on December 6, 1658, he states: "Did the Lord not agree that women should enter his company? Yes. Did he not lead them to perfection and to the assistance of the poor? Yes. If, therefore, our Lord did that, he who did everything for our instruction, should we not consider it right to do the same thing? . . . So God is served equally by both sexes" (SV XII, 86-87).

But the purpose of this brief note is to focus not so much on Saint Vincent's way of relating to women as on one of his ways of relating to Jesus. To put it simply: While he comes among us as a man, Jesus, for Vincent, also has a maternal face.

Vincent writes to Nicolas Etienne, a cleric, on January 30, 1656: "May it please God to grant the Company to which you belong the grace . . . to have a deep love of Jesus Christ, who is our father, our mother and our all" (SV V, 534).

The following year, he writes to a priest of the Mission whose mother had died, saying that he has recommended to the prayers of the Community "not only the deceased mother, but also her living son so that the Lord himself might take the place of his father and mother and might be his consolation" (SV VI, 444).

In 1659, upon the death of the mother of Marin Baucher, a brother in the Congregation, he writes: "I ask our Lord to take the place of your father and mother" (SV VIII, 55).

The most striking passage of all appears in a letter to Mathurine Guérin, written on March 3, 1660, just after the death of Monsieur Portail and just before that of Louise de Marillac:

> Certainly it is the great secret of the spiritual life to abandon to him all whom we love, while abandoning ourselves to whatever he wishes, with perfect confidence that everything will go better in that way. It is for that reason that it is said that everything works for the good of those who serve God. Let us serve him, therefore, my Sister, but let us serve him according to his pleasure, allowing him to do as he wishes. He will take the role of father and mother for us. He will be your consolation and your strength and finally the reward of your love. (SV VIII, 256)

Two ideas emerge from these texts:

1. Vincent sees the maternal face of Jesus

Saint Vincent wrote to the Vincentians and the Daughters of Charity, with his characteristic simplicity, about both the father and the mother in the human personality in Jesus. In doing so, he makes it evident that he had appropriated into his own spirituality a basic scriptural truth.

The Old Testament unabashedly depicts God as a mother. "Can a mother forget her infant, be without tenderness for the child of her womb? Even should she forget, I will never forget you" (Is 49:15). Yahweh complains: "I have looked away, and kept silence, I have said nothing, holding myself in. But now, I cry out as a woman in labor, gasping and panting" (Is 42:14). The Psalmist rests in God with deep confidence: "I have stilled and quieted my soul like a weaned child. Like a weaned child on its mother's lap, so is my soul within me" (Ps 131:2).

In the New Testament, Luke's gospel likewise does not hesitate to use the image of a mother in describing Jesus' deep sorrow over the infidelity of Jerusalem. Jesus laments: "How often I wanted to gather your children together as a mother bird collects her young under her wings, but you refused" (Lk 13:34).

In reflecting on the scriptures and seeing Jesus as a mother, Vincent was surely not alone among the saints. One is reminded of the striking words of Anselm of Canterbury:

> But you too, good Jesus, are you not also a mother?
> Are you not a mother who like a hen gathers her chicks beneath her wings? . . .
> And you, my soul, dead in yourself,
> run under the wings of Jesus your mother
> and lament your griefs under his feathers.
> Ask that your wounds may be healed
> and that, comforted you may live again.
> Christ, my mother, you gather your chickens under your wings;
> This dead chicken of yours puts himself under those wings. . . .
> Warm your chicken, give life to your dead one, justify your sinner.[3]

In this age, when, under Jungian influence, people often speak of the *animus* and the *anima* within us,[4] and when there is considerable writing on a male and female spirituality,[5] it is interesting to note how naturally Saint Vincent wrote of both the father and the mother in Jesus.

---

3. Cf. *The Prayers and Meditations of Saint Anselm*, translated by S. Benedicta Ward (New York: Penguin, 1973), 153-56, as quoted in Elizabeth Johnson, *She Who Is* (New York: Crossroad, 1992), 150.
4. While commonly employed, Jung's analysis is much disputed today. Cf. Sandra Schneiders, *Beyond Patching* (Mahwah: Paulist Press, 1991), 85-89; also, John Carmody, *Toward a Male Spirituality* (Mystic: Twenty-Third Publications, 1989) 94-108. Carmody wisely comments that "no single formula will set the sexes into tidy traffic patterns" (p. 94). So far, it seems to me, we have not come up with a proper analytical tool for speaking of masculine and feminine qualities, since it is not easy to discern what is in us "by nature" and what is "learned." Nonetheless, almost everyone continues to use some conceptual framework for discussing this question. Non-scientific frameworks are usually based on our concrete experience of the persons we know. For a very interesting discussion of these issues, cf. E. Johnson, *Consider Jesus* 47-57.
5. In addition to the works cited in the note above, cf. also William O'Malley, "The Grail Quest: Male Spirituality," *America*, vol. 166, n. 16 (May 9, 1992), 402-06; O'Malley, "A Male's View of Female Spirituality," *Human Development*, vol. 14, n. 3 (Fall 1993), 33-38; Sally Cunneen, "What if the Church is a Mother?" *America*, vol. 165, n. 17 (November 30, 1991), 407-10. Cf. also Patrick Arnold, *Wildmen, Warriors, and Kings. Masculine Spirituality and the Bible* (New York: Crossroad, 1992).

2. Vincent's view of providence has a maternal face

All of the letters cited above in which Vincent describes Jesus as a mother deal with tragic events. In some of them he appeals explicitly to the need to trust in providence; in others, the appeal is implicit. In each case, he is saying basically to his correspondent: God reveals, in Christ, that he loves you like a father, but also like a mother—like your own mother or like Louise de Marillac, the "mother" of the Daughters of Charity.

He is concerned to assure the readers of these letters that God accompanies them, in Christ, as a mother accompanies her child, that he is concerned about their future, and that his love is warm and ever present.

In a conference given on June 9, 1658, he tells the Daughters: "To have confidence in providence means that we should hope that God takes care of those who serve him, as a husband takes care of his wife or a father of his child. That is how—and far more truly—God takes care of us. We have only to abandon ourselves to his guidance, as the Rule says, just as 'a little child does to its nurse.' If she puts it on her right arm, the child is quite content; if she moves him over to her left, he doesn't care, he is quite satisfied provided he has her breast. We should then have the same confidence in divine providence, seeing that it takes care of all that concerns us, just as a nursing mother takes care of her baby" (SV X, 503).

Reflecting on the texts cited in this brief note, one might suggest that Saint Vincent's recognition of the father and mother in Jesus enabled him to develop both the father and the mother within himself. Like the Jesus he meditated on, he had a full share of the qualities usually associated[6] with the "fatherly" side of the human personality (showing anger in the face of injustice, demonstrating formidable organizational skills in the service of the poor), but like him too, he could turn a warm, compassionate, provident "maternal face" toward the members of his congregations and toward the poor.

---

6. As stated in note 4 above, I use the terminology "qualities usually associated" with being male or female purposely, since such attribution is quite culturally conditioned.

Mental Prayer, Yesterday and Today: The Vincentian Tradition

Saint Vincent and Mental Prayer

Some preliminary considerations

I use the phrase "mental prayer" purposely in this chapter, rather than "meditation." Saint Vincent rarely used the verb *méditer*. He ordinarily employed the phrase *faire oraison*.[1] I also recognize, however, the limitations of the phrase "mental prayer." Saint Vincent aimed not at a mental exercise, but at affective prayer and contemplation. The method he proposed, which involved use of the mind in focusing on a certain subject, was meant merely as a *method*. It aimed at higher things.

Few things were as important as prayer in Saint Vincent's mind.[2] Speaking to the Missionaries, he declares:

> Give me a man of prayer and he will be capable of everything. He may say with the apostle, "I can do all things in him who strengthens me." The Congregation will last as long as it faithfully carries out the practice of prayer, which is like an impregnable rampart shielding the missionaries from all manner of attack (SV XI, 83).[3]

---

1. Actually he uses *faire oraison* thirty times, while using *méditer* only six times in his writings, conferences or prayers.
2. There have been a number of important studies on Saint Vincent's teaching about prayer. I offer here a brief, selected bibliography that may be helpful to the reader. André Dodin, *En Prière avec Monsieur Vincent* (Paris: Desclée de Brouwer, 1982); Joseph Leonard, *Saint Vincent de Paul and Mental Prayer* (New York: Benziger Brothers, 1925); Arnaud D'Agnel, *Saint Vincent de Paul, Maître d'Oraison* (Paris: Pierre Téqui, 1929); Jacques Delarue, *L'Idéal Missionaire du Prêtre d'après Saint Vincent de Paul* (Paris: Missions Lazaristes, 1947); Antonino Oracajo and Miguel Pérez Flores, *San Vicente de Paúl II, Espiritualidad y Seleccion de Escritos* (Madrid: BAC, 1981) 120-135. Today, moreover, there are various collections of the prayers of Saint Vincent, in most of the modern languages. These are similar to those found in Dodin's work cited above.
3. Cf. also III, 539; IX, 416; X, 583.

It is interesting to note that the word he uses here is *oraison*. He is speaking about the importance of mental prayer. Saint Vincent states quite forcefully on a number of occasions, moreover, that the failure to rise early in the morning to join the community in prayer will be the reason why missionaries fail to persevere in their vocation.[4]

To encourage his sons and daughters to pray, he used many of the similes commonly found in the spiritual writers of his day. He tells them that prayer is for the soul what food is for the body (SV IX, 416). It is a "fountain of youth" by which we are invigorated (SV IX, 217). It is a mirror in which we see all our blotches and begin to adorn ourselves in order to be pleasing to God (SV IX, 417). It is refreshment in the midst of difficult daily work in the service of the poor (SV IX, 416). He tells the missionaries that it is a sermon that we preach to ourselves (SV XI, 84). It is a resource book for the preacher in which he can find the eternal truths that he shares with God's people (SV VII, 156). It is a gentle dew that refreshes the soul every morning, he tells the Daughters of Charity (SV IX, 402.)

He urged Saint Louise to form the young sisters very well in prayer (SV IV, 47). He himself gave many practical conferences to them on the subject. It is evident from these conferences that many had difficulties in engaging in mental prayer (cf. SV IV, 390; IX, 216). He assures them that it is really quite easy! It is like having a conversation for half an hour. He states, with some irony, that people are usually glad to talk with the king. We should be all the more glad to have a chance to talk with God (SV IX, 115). He gives numerous examples of those who have learned to pray, in all classes of society: peasant girls, servants, soldiers, actors and actresses, lawyers, statesmen, fashionable women and noblemen of the court, judges. In the various conferences that he gave upon the occasion of the death of Daughters of Charity, he often alluded to their prayerfulness. Speaking of Joan Dalmagne on January 15, 1645 he observed: "She walked in the presence of God" (SV IX, 180).

He defines *oraison* as "an elevation of the mind to God by which the soul detaches itself, as it were, from itself so as to seek God in himself. It is a conversation with God, an intercourse of the spirit, in which God interiorly teaches it what it should know and do, and in which the soul says to God what he himself teaches it to ask for" (SV IX, 419).

---

4. SV III, 538; IX, 29, 416; X, 566, 583.

Among the dispositions necessary for prayer he lists principally humility, indifference, and mortification. The humble recognize their absolute dependence on God. They come to prayer filled with gratitude for God's gifts and a recognition of their own limitations and sinfulness (SV X, 128-29). Indifference enables the person to live in a state of detachment and union with the will of God, so that in coming to prayer he or she seeks only to know and to do what God will reveal (SV XII, 231). Saint Vincent often returns to the need for mortification in order to pray well, particularly in getting out of bed promptly in the morning. He tells the Daughters on August 2, 1640 that our bodies are like jackasses: accustomed to the low road, they will always follow it (SV IX, 28-29).

The principal subject of prayer, for Vincent, is the life and teaching of Jesus (SV XII, 113). He emphasized that we must focus again and again on the humanity of Jesus.[5] He meditated on what Jesus did and taught in the scriptures (CR I, 1), calling special attention, among Jesus' teachings, to the Sermon on the Mount (SV XII, 125-27). Most of all, however, he recommended the passion and cross of Jesus as the subject of prayer.[6]

Saint Vincent did not hesitate to recommend the use of images and books of prayer (SV IX, 32-33; X, 569). Among the latter, he was especially fond of the *Imitation of Christ*,[7] Francis de Sales' *Introduction to a Devout Life*[8] and *Treatise on the Love of God*,[9] Busée's meditations,[10] and Louis of Granada's, *The Sinner's Guide, Memorial of the Christian Life*, and his *Catechism*,[11] as well as Jean Souffarand's *L'Année Chrétienne* (SV VI, 632). It is evident that the Vincentians and Daughters used other meditation books too, such as those of Saint-Jure (SV IX, 109) and Suffrand (SV VI, 632).

Affective prayer and contemplation

Saint Vincent puts great stress on affective prayer, but, in doing so, he is very reserved about working oneself up into a highly emotional state.

5. André Dodin, *En prière avec Monsieur Vincent* (Paris, Desclée de Brouwer, 1982) 197.
6. SV IX, 32, 217; X, 569; cf. also IV, 139, 590; I, 134; cf. X, 569: "Is it not a good meditation to have the thought of the passion and death of our Lord always in one's heart?"
7. SV I, 382; V, 297.
8. SV I, 155-56, 398; III, 551; IX, 13, 44, 50; XII, 2; XIII, 81, 435, 822.
9. SV I, 86; XIII, 71, 822.
10. SV I, 197; III, 283; IV, 105, 620; VII, 66, 274; VIII, 501.
11. SV I, 198, 382; cf. III, 282.

He recognizes that the feelings aroused by mental prayer (for example, sorrow at Christ's passion) can be quite advantageous, even though, in themselves, they are not the heart of prayer. The "affections" that he focuses on are geared primarily toward acts of the will. "Affective" love should lead to "effective" love. Our affective acts should tend to become simpler and simpler, leading eventually to contemplation.

Contemplation is a gift from God. While we engage in mental prayer and affective prayer by our own choice, we engage in contemplation only when grasped by God (SV IX, 420). In contemplation we "taste and see" that the Lord is good. Such contemplation, while a pure gift from God, is for Saint Vincent the normal issue of the spiritual life. It is quite evident from his conferences that he regarded some of the Daughters of Charity as contemplatives. He encouraged them to become other Saint Teresas (SV IX, 424). On July 24, 1660, when he spoke about the virtues of Louise de Marillac, he rejoiced at a sister's description of Louise: "As soon as she was alone, she was in a state of prayer" (SV X, 728).

The method

The method that Saint Vincent teaches is basically the same as the one given by Francis de Sales.[12] He makes only slight modifications. While putting very high value on affective prayer, he insists again and again on the need for practical resolutions. Particularly in his conferences to the Daughters, there is a lovely mingling of spiritual wisdom and common sense. He is more restrained than Francis de Sales when speaking about the use of the imagination. He warns over and over again about regarding prayer as a speculative study. He cautions about its becoming an occasion for vanity or for "beautiful thoughts" that lead nowhere.

Saint Vincent suggested, by way of preparation for prayer, reading in the evening some points that will stimulate mental prayer the next morning (SV IX, 426; X, 590-91; XII, 64). He also regarded peaceful silence in the house at night and in the morning as the basic atmosphere for prayer (SV IX, 3-7, 120, 219).

The method he proposes can be presented schematically as follows (cf. SV IX, 420; X, 573; XI, 406):

---

12. Cf. SV X, 587; cf. Francis de Sales, *Introduction to the Devout Life*, "The Second Part of the Introduction," chs. 1-10; *Treatise on the Love of God* 1.IV, chs. 1-15; cf. also A. Dodin, *François de Sales/Vincent de Paul, les deux amis* (Paris: O.E.I.L., 1984) 65-67.

a. *Preparation*. First, you place yourself in the presence of God, through one of several ways: by considering yourself present before our Lord in the Blessed Sacrament, by thinking of God reigning in heaven or within yourself, by reflecting on his omnipresence, by pondering his presence in the souls of the just. Then you ask God's help to pray well; you also petition the help of the Blessed Virgin, your guardian angel, and patron saints. Then you choose a subject for meditation, such as a mystery of religion, a moral or theological virtue, or some maxim of our Lord.

b. *Body*. You begin to consider the subject (e.g., the passion of Christ). If the subject is a virtue, you reflect on the motives for loving and practicing the virtue. If it is a mystery, you think of the truth contained in the mystery. As you reflect, you seek to arouse acts of the will (e.g., love of Christ who suffered so much for us), by which, under the impulse of grace, you express love of God, sorrow for sin, or desire for perfection. You then make concrete resolutions.

c. *Conclusion*. You thank God for this time of meditation, and for the graces granted during prayer. You place before God the resolutions made. Then, you offer to God the whole prayer that you have made, with a request for help in carrying out the resolutions.

Two related teachings

Saint Vincent encouraged the members of his two communities to share their prayer with one another. He recommended that this be done every two or three days (SV IX, 421-22). He had learned this practice from others. Saint Philip Neri's Oratorians, for example, were already engaging in repetition of prayer (cf. SV XI, 293-95). When Saint Vincent recommends it to the Daughters, moreover, he cites the example of Madame Acarie (SV IX, 4). In his conferences to the Daughters, we find wonderful examples of the simplicity with which they shared their thoughts in prayer. He often notes, in addition, how well the brothers in the Congregation shared their prayer (SV IX, 421-22). He tells the Missionaries on August 15, 1659 that shared prayer has been a great grace in the Company (SV XII, 288).

Another teaching of Saint Vincent, frequently found in his conferences to the Daughters of Charity, is the practice of "leaving God for God" (SV IX, 319; X, 95, 226, 541, 542, 595, 693). The poor often arrived unexpectedly and made urgent demands on the Daughters. Saint Vincent encouraged them to respond, telling them that they would be leaving God whom they were encountering in prayer in order to find him in the person of the poor. At the same time, Saint Vincent urged the Daughters and the Vincentians never to miss prayer (SV VIII, 368-39; IX, 426). It is striking that, though he was very firm about the rule of rising early in the morning and never missing prayer, Saint Vincent brings his usual common sense to the application of the rule. He tells the Daughters: "You see, charity is above all the rules and it is necessary that everything be related to it. She is a noble woman. You should do what she orders. In such a case it is to leave God for God. God calls you to prayer, and at the same time he calls you to the poor sick person. That is called leaving God for God" (SV X, 595).

Horizon-Shifts That Have Taken Place Between Saint Vincent's Day and Ours

Three changes in horizon significantly influence attitudes toward prayer today.

The liturgical movement

Saint Vincent was very concerned about liturgy. He noted that priests often celebrated Mass badly and that they hardly knew how to hear confessions. As part of the retreats for ordinands, he prescribed that they receive instruction on celebrating the liturgy well. But, within this positive context, he was still very much a man of his time. The emphasis of the era was on the exact observance of rubrics. There was little stress on liturgy as "communal celebration," with the active participation of all the faithful. Much of liturgy was private, as in the daily celebration of individual Masses, perhaps with a server. Liturgical celebrations were often regarded more as part of the priest's "personal piety," rather than of his leadership of a local community in prayer.

The liturgical movement, Vatican II, and the implementation of the Constitution on the Liturgy have changed attitudes and practices dramatically. The Constitution on the Liturgy proclaimed liturgy as the summit toward which the action of the Church tends and at the same time the fountain from which all virtue emanates.[13] Of course, this implies liturgy

---

13. *Sacrosanctum Concilium* 10.

is not all of prayer. As a "summit" it must rest on a solid foundation. Nonetheless, as is evident from the enormous energy that the Church has invested in liturgical reform over the last thirty years, liturgy plays an extremely important part in the life of the Christian community. Today we speak of a "liturgical piety."

Renewed interest in personal prayer

At the very same time, and not just among Christians, enthusiasm for personal prayer is being revived. Courses in seminaries, novitiates, and institutes for spirituality are focusing on some of the classics that teach methods of prayer; for example, *The Cloud of Unknowing*,[14] *The Introduction to the Devout Life*,[15] *The Way of a Pilgrim*.[16] There has been renewed research and interest in the prayer of oriental religions and the use of mantras. Thomas Merton called our attention to the rich tradition of the oriental Church in regard to contemplation and the "wisdom of the desert."[17] Karl Rahner too focused on the central place of prayer in Christian spirituality.[18]

Concrete signs of this renewed interest are evident in prayer groups, the charismatic movement, the rise of new communities, and the updated practices of many already existing religious communities.

From the personal to the interpersonal to the social

One of the persistent dangers in Christian spirituality is "intimism," a kind of piety in which the individual becomes absorbed in himself and gradually cut off from interpersonal and social responsibilities. The person remains passive, almost immune from the contagion of the world.

Saint Vincent certainly avoided that temptation! But some of his contemporaries did not. Various forms of quietism were condemned in his day.[19] Quietists stressed the exclusive efficacy of grace in a corrupt

---

14. Anonymous, *The Cloud of Unknowing* (New York: Doubleday, 1973).

15. Francis de Sales, *Introduction to the Devout Life*, translated and edited by John Ryan (Garden City: Doubleday, 1972).

16. Anonymous, *The Way of a Pilgrim* (New York: Doubleday, 1978).

17. Thomas Merton, *Contemplative Prayer* (Garden City: Doubleday, 1971).

18. Cf. K. Rahner, *Spiritual Exercises* (New York: Herder and Herder, 1966).

19. For an interesting treatment, cf. L. Dupré, "Jansenism and Quietism," *Christian Spirituality III, Post-Reformation and Modern* (New York: Crossroad, 1989) 130-41.

world and advocated total abandonment to God's action, with the individual remaining passive.

Much of the piety of Saint Vincent's day, even when it took forms healthier than quietism, tended to be rather individualistic. In the twentieth century we have experienced greater emphasis on the interpersonal. Personalist philosophy has had profound influence on contemporary thought and practice. Martin Buber made the "I-Thou" a part of our vocabulary today.[20]

Beyond that, we have seen an increasing emphasis on the social and societal, with a growing consciousness of the interrelatedness of all persons and of all human reality.[21] The Pastoral Constitution on the Church in the Modern World proclaims that the joys and hopes, the sorrows and anguish of contemporary men and women, especially the poor and those suffering affliction, are the joys and hopes, the sorrows and anguish of Christ's disciples too.[22] The social encyclicals over the last century have more and more emphasized Christians' responsibility for justice in the world.[23] The Church's preferential option for the poor is stressed again and again.[24] Christians are encouraged to develop a global worldview and to play their part in working for the "transformation of the world."[25]

These three horizon-shifts, of course, in no way negate the importance of mental prayer. Rather, they set the context for it. If liturgy is the "source and summit" of the Church's prayerful action, then reflection on the mystery of Christ, the gospels, and the human condition is one of its foundation stones. If contemporary men and women, especially the young, are showing renewed interest in various prayer forms, then mental prayer, or "meditation," is finding a significant place among these. If there is a sharp tendency to criticize "intimism" in spirituality and a movement toward emphasis on the interpersonal and the social, then these are ways of broadening the horizons of mental prayer, as well as sharpening its focus.

20. Cf. M. Buber, *The Way of Man According to the Teaching of Hasidism* (Secaucus: Citadel, 1966).
21. Cf. *Sollicitudo Rei Socialis*, 26.
22. *Gaudium et Spes*, 1.
23. Synod of Bishops, 1971, *Justice in the World* in *AAS* LXIII (1971) 924.
24. Cf. *Sollicitudo Rei Socialis*, 42.
25. *AAS* LXIII (1971) 924.

Mental Prayer Today

Karl Rahner puts the matter very clearly: "Personal experience of God is the heart of all spirituality."[26] Saint Vincent knew this, so he encouraged the confreres and the Daughters of Charity again and again to pray. The Common Rule which he wrote for the Congregation of the Mission called for an hour of mental prayer each day.[27] The Vincentian Constitutions of 1984 have modified this, speaking of an hour of personal prayer daily according to the tradition of Saint Vincent (C 47).[28] While this prescription is clearly broader than that of the Common Rule, it surely involves a significant period of mental prayer.[29] The original Rule of the Daughters of Charity demanded two half-hour periods;[30] their present Constitutions[31] call for one hour of *oraison* daily.

Today, especially in light of the second horizon-shift mentioned above, a rich variety of methods might be proposed as a help in mental prayer. On the following page I have grouped these schematically under four headings.

---

26. K. Rahner, "The Spirituality of the Church of the Future," in *Theological Investigations* XX, 150.
27. CR X, 7; cf. also, SV I, 563; VIII, 368.
28. For a clear presentation of the history and an explanation of the context of Article 47, cf. Miguel Pérez Flores, "Oración personal diaria, en privado o en común, durante una hora," *Anales* 95 (#3; March 1987) 162-68.
29. *Statutes of the Congregation of the Mission* 19; henceforth S.
30. *Rules of the Daughters of Charity* IX, 1-2.
31. *Constitutions of the Daughters of Charity* 2.14; cf. also, SV IX, 29.

Prayer of the Mind	Prayer of the Imagination	Prayer of the Heart	Lectio Divina
1. Nature—What is humility? • search the scriptures • search the writings of Saint Vincent • search some classical or contemporary writer	1. Activate the imagination by focusing on a gospel scene.	1. At the beginning of prayer, take a minute or two to quiet down and then move in faith to God dwelling within you.	1. *Lectio*—What is the text actually saying?
2. Motives—Why should I be humble? • search the scriptures • search the writings of Saint Vincent • search some classical or contemporary writer	2. Take the part of one of the persons in the scene. 3. Ask questions. • What? • Who? • Why? • How?	2. After resting a bit in the center of faith-full love, take up a simple word or phrase that expresses your response and begin to let it repeat itself within you.	2. *Meditatio*— What does it say *to me?* 3. *Oratio*—Speaking with God, using the text as a starting point.
3. Means—How can I grow in humility? • doing humble things • allowing myself to be evangelized by the poor • focusing on the good in others rather than their faults • developing a servant's attitude	4. "Be there" in your imagination, returning to the scene as a bystander. 5. If the meditation is on a teaching, read the text three times, pausing after each reading.	3. Whenever in the course of prayer you become aware of anything else, gently return to the prayer word. 4. At the end of prayer, take several minutes to come out, praying the Our Father.	4. *Contemplatio*—Becoming absorbed in the person of Jesus.

Let me illustrate each of these methods briefly.

1. Prayer of the mind

This is basically the method that Saint Vincent proposes. A Vincentian using this method to meditate on humility would proceed as follows:

a. Nature—What is humility?

He would search the scriptures for sections that speak of humility. He might reflect, for example, on Luke 1:46, the Magnificat, and Mary's gratitude for God's many gifts. Or he might turn to Philippians 2:5, in which Jesus takes on the form of a servant, humbling himself and becoming obedient even to death. Or he might focus on Mark 9:33, where Jesus speaks about the humility required of leaders. He asks: What is this humility that the gospels recommend? What does it consist of? Little by little, he may come to formulate personal convictions, such as: Humility is a recognition of my creatureliness, that I am totally dependent upon God. It is a recognition of my redeemedness, that I sin often and need God's help to be converted. I am slow to get excited about gospel values. I speak too lightly about others' negative points. I comply too easily with unjust social structures. But I also trust that the Lord forgives me eagerly, and I have great confidence in his power to heal me. Humility is also gratitude for God's many gifts. The humble person cries out with Mary, "He who is mighty has done great things for me. Holy is his name" (Lk 1:49). It involves a servant's attitude. We are called, like Jesus, "not to be served but to serve" (Mt 20:28). Humility also entails allowing myself to be evangelized by the poor, "our Lords and Masters," as Saint Vincent liked to call them. It involves listening well and learning.

Another approach would be for him to search the writings of Saint Vincent, or the Vincentian tradition, concerning humility. He might look at the Common Rules II, 6-7 or X, 13-14, and ponder the steps Saint Vincent describes for acquiring humility. He could also look into what classical or contemporary writers say on the subject.

The starting-point for this method is thinking, reasoning. This is very important at some stage in the spiritual life, since a person must think through, in a reasonable way, his personal values and what they concretely mean; otherwise he might wind up with a fuzzy view of the gospels. It is important that a member of the community be able to articulate, in a way that is coherent both for himself and for others, what his values are.

b. Motives—Why should I be humble?

The same sources mentioned above provide ample motives. Matthew 18:4 says that the humble are of the greatest importance in the kingdom of God. Philippians 2:9 says that it is precisely because of this attitude, which is found in Christ Jesus, that God highly exalted him. Saint Vincent states that humility is the core of evangelical perfection and the heart of the spiritual life (CR II, 7). He also states that it engenders charity (SV X, 530). Contemporary writers emphasize the need for us to recognize our utter dependence on God and to sing out our praise and gratitude for his gifts.

Once again here the emphasis is on thinking and reasoning, but these are geared toward acts of the will; e.g., trust in the Lord, love, gratitude, submission to his will.

c. Means—How can I grow in humility?

The missionary who is meditating might come up with a number of means, as described in the scheme above.

In all of this it is important to recognize that the goal is not merely reflection, mental exercise, or a sharpening of one's reasoning or verbal skills. The immediate goal is affective prayer, letting one's heart go and entering into conversation with the Lord. This conversation should result in concrete resolutions and change of life. It will, if we are faithful, become simpler, less verbal, and will lead to contemplation, where more and more God seizes the heart.

Prayer of the mind is very important at various stages in a person's life. At the time of initial formation, especially, it is imperative that a young man or woman come to grips with the *meaning* of gospel values. Unless the person can articulate those values in a way that makes sense both to himself and to others, the gospels will eventually seem irrelevant. There is a whole series of topics that a Vincentian or Daughter of Charity might very profitably ponder. In fact, Saint Vincent led his communities through similar topics by asking them to engage in mental prayer and then joining with them in conferences and repetitions of prayer. At different stages in our initial and ongoing formation we might gain much by using prayer of the mind on the following themes:

— Jesus' deep human love
— his relationship with God as Father
— the kingdom he preached
— his community with the apostles
— his prayer
— sin
— Jesus' eagerness to forgive and his healing power
— his attitude as a servant
— his love of truth and simplicity
— his humility
— his thirst for justice
— his longing for peace
— his struggle with temptation
— the cross
— the resurrection
— Jesus' obedience to the Father's will
— Jesus' gentleness and meekness
— mortification
— apostolic zeal
— poverty
— celibacy
— obedience
— Jesus' joy and thanksgiving.

2. Prayer of the imagination

This is basically the Ignatian method. A Daughter of Charity using this method to meditate on the passion narratives, for example, might proceed as follows:

a. Activate the imagination

She goes, in her imagination, to the scene. She looks at the local setting, Jerusalem, teeming with people who have come to celebrate the Pasch. She tries to hear the sounds of the crowd, to feel the heat of the day, to sense the smells, to taste what the participants might have tasted. She looks around the scene to see who is there: the faces of excited pilgrims, the Pharisees, the scribes, the Romans, Jesus and his followers. She listens to what they are saying. She feels what they are feeling. She notes their personal characteristics.

b. Take the part of one of the persons in the scene

Taking the part of Jesus, she imagines, even in the smallest details, what he is thinking, feeling, doing. She loves with him. She grieves with him. She has compassion with him. She aches with him. She is abandoned with him.

c. Ask questions

She puts a number of questions to herself. Which person am I in the scene? Why? What is it about Jesus here that captivates me, that draws me to love him? Is there some way he would like me to live out what he is doing in this scene? Who? What? Why? When? How? For whom? Does it all make a difference?

d. "Be there" in your imagination

The meditator returns to the scene, but this time as a bystander. She simply watches, listens, and lets the scene work upon her. She stands by the cross beside Mary and John. She takes her place with the spectators in the crowd. She is near Peter or the penitent thief.

e. Read the text three times, pausing after each reading

The first time she asks: What did Jesus *say*? Was I concentrating? She might examine some commentary too to find the precise meaning of his words. Who are the "poor in spirit"? What is the "reign of God" promised to them?

The second time she tries to listen more attentively. What does Jesus *mean*? What does he mean *for me*? Often the poor do not seem happy to me. Why does Jesus say that they are? Am I among the poor in spirit? Am I really happy?

The third time she speaks directly with Jesus or with his Father about the text. She may even visualize the conversation, sitting with Jesus and his followers by a fire at the lakeside in the evening, feeling some awe, but at the same time deep love. She says to him: "Lord, help me to understand what this is all about. I really want to be poor in spirit, to rely completely on you. I know you love me. Help me, please."

3. Prayer of the heart

Today this is commonly called centering prayer. Its classical expression is found in works like the *Cloud of Unknowing* or *The Way of a Pilgrim*. One of its well-known contemporary proponents is Basil Pennington.[32] It can be summarized in four rules.

Rule 1—*At the beginning of prayer, take a minute or two to quiet down and then move on in faith to God dwelling within you.*

A lay person or member of a community engaging in this type of prayer would seek first to find a quiet place. She then assumes a relaxed position. She might try to breathe deeply and regularly in order to calm down and then begin to focus on God. As a help, she might direct her attention to the words of Galatians 2:20: "I live, now not I, but Christ lives in me. Of course, I still live my human life, but it is a life of faith in the Son of God, who loved me and gave himself for me."

Rule 2—*After resting a bit at the center in faith-full love, take up a simple single word or phrase that expresses your response and begin to let it repeat itself within you.*

She tries to do this simply, with no strain. She chooses a word or phrase that expresses what is deepest in her heart: God, love, the Jesus prayer. She repeats it slowly, gently: "Lord Jesus Christ, Son of God, have mercy on me, a sinner." Or perhaps: "Speak, Lord, for your servant is listening" (1 Sam 3:9). Or: "I love you, Lord; thank you for your love." There are many possible mantric phrases: "There is nothing I shall want" (Ps 23). "A pure heart create for me" (Ps 51). "Give me the joy of your help" (Ps 51). "Live through love in his presence" (Eph 1:3-12). "Your love is better than life" (Ps 63). "You are precious in my eyes" (Is 43:1-5). "I came that they may have life" (Jn 10:1-10). "Be still! Know that I am God" (Ps 46:10).

Rule 3—*Whenever in the course of prayer you become aware of anything else, gently return to the prayer word.*

Other thoughts and images always intrude. The pray-er, for example, might find herself examining the prayer word for its meaning, but this should be avoided. She simply repeats the word and lets her heart go to God.

---

32. Cf. M. Basil Pennington, *Call to the Center* (Hyde Park: New City Press, 1995), 7-14; "Centering Prayer: Refining the Rules," *Review for Religious,* vol. 46, n.3 (May-June 1986) 386-93.

Rule 4—*At the end of prayer, take several minutes to come out, praying the Our Father.*
This type of prayer moves deeply into interiority. It is not good to be jarred out of it (this can be like waking up startled from a deep sleep). Rather, the pray-er should relax, be silent for a few minutes, say the Lord's Prayer, recalling God's presence, and then conclude.

4. Lectio divina

A fourth method of prayer, one commonly used in the Church's long monastic tradition, is *lectio divina.* Classical expressions of this method can be found in the writings of the great monastic founders.

The scriptures are the primary, though by no means exclusive, source of *lectio divina.* Sacred scripture is central in the life of the Church. The Constitution on the Liturgy tells us that "in the sacred books the Father who is in heaven meets his children with great love and speaks with them; and the force in the Word of God is so great that it remains the support and energy of the Church, the strength of faith for her children, the food of the soul, the pure and perennial source of spiritual life."[33] The Bible is, for all believers, the water that gives life to the aridity of human existence (Is 55:10-11), the food that is sweeter than honey (Ps 19:11), the hammer that shatters hardened indifference (Jer 23:29), and the two-edged sword that pierces obstinate refusal (Heb 4:12).

Saint Vincent's prayer and spirituality were deeply rooted in the scriptures. Abelly, his first biographer, said of him: "He seemed to suck meaning from passages of the scriptures as a baby sucks milk from its mother. And he extracted the core and substance from the scriptures so as to be strengthened and have his soul nourished by them . . . and he did this in such a way that in all his words and actions he appeared to be filled with Jesus Christ."[34] He also often recommended the use of other books to aid in praying.

Cardinal Carlo Maria Martini, the Archbishop of Milan, frequently proposes the use of *lectio divina* in his talks to young people[35] He describes its methodology as follows:

33. *Dei Verbum*, 21.
34. Louis Abelly, *Life of the Venerable Servant*, III:72-73.
35. C. Martini, "Educati dalla Parola, Meditazione del Cardinale Arcivescovo Carlo Maria Martini," *Annali della Missione* 100, n. 3 (July-September 1993) 203-17.

a. *Lectio.* A young person should read the biblical text again and again, trying to understand it in its immediate context and within the context of the scriptures as a whole. The focus here is on the question: What is the *text* actually saying? Martini suggests to young people that they use a pen to underline significant nouns or verbs or adjectives or adverbs and that they make marginal notes. The text is read slowly so that the reader lets the Bible speak to him. It will often reveal different things at different times in the reader's life.

b. *Meditatio.* If the emphasis in *lectio* is on what the text itself says, then the accent in *meditatio* is on a further question: What does it say *to me*? What are the values, the dispositions, the changes in my life, that it is demanding? What is it saying *today*, in the here and now, as the living word of God, as the voice of the Spirit?

c. *Oratio.* Here the focus is on praying. The biblical message arouses a response. It may be fear of the Lord because I am so far from living out what the word of God is actually asking of me. Or it may be adoration of the living God who reveals himself so graciously to me in his word. It may be a cry for help to put the word of God into practice better. In all cases *oratio* consists of speaking with God, using the text and its message as a starting point. The focus of *oratio* is: What does the word of God *move me to say*?

d. *Contemplatio.* Prayer becomes *contemplatio* when it goes beyond a particular passage and becomes absorbed in the person of Jesus, who is present behind and in every page of the scriptures. At this point prayer is no longer an exercise of the mind but is praise and silence before the one who is being revealed, who speaks to me, who listens to me, who is present to me as a friend, as a healer, as a Savior. In *contemplatio*, the pray-er tastes the word of God and experiences God's life within himself or herself.

Cardinal Martini adds that those who enter into *lectio divina* will inevitably, as the Fathers of the Church often pointed out, experience four movements in the process. Actually, these terms, or similar ones, are commonly used to describe what goes on as one employs other methods too; e.g., Ignatian prayer.

a. *Consolatio.* Here one tastes God's goodness, the grandeur of the world he created, his redeeming presence. The pray-er rejoices in the mystery of Christ, in God's love, in the beatitudes. Consolation is the joy of the Holy Spirit that fills the heart as we contemplate the mystery of Christ revealed in the scriptures.

b. *Discretio.* Consolation gives rise to spiritual discernment, the capacity to evaluate the various inner movements that I sense in my heart, to distinguish the good from the bad, to recognize my conflicting motives. It is the ability to identify, within my present situation (personal, ecclesial, social, civil), those things that resonate with the gospel message and those things that are discordant with it. It is the capacity to grasp the better, the more, the spirit of the beatitudes. It is the ability to think more and more as Christ did.

c. *Deliberatio.* Discernment leads to decision-making, life-choices, or a commitment to act according to the word of God. It is in the phase of *deliberatio* that *lectio divina* gives birth to concrete judgments based on the gospel.

d. *Actio.* This step is the fruit of one's prayer. The pray-er performs works of justice, charitable service, attentive listening, labor, sacrifice, forgiveness.

Some Practical Rules for Praying

I offer these "rules" for the use of those who seek to pray daily. They are not abstract principles; nor are they conclusions which are provable by some deductive method. They are simply a group of practical rules that experience teaches are helpful for those who want to pray. While I take responsibility for their formulation, I owe a deep debt of gratitude to others who have taught them to me.

1. Faithful prayer requires discipline. Saint Vincent alluded to this when he spoke of mortification as a prerequisite for prayer. It is important to fix a prayer time and to have a prayer place. Likewise, it is most helpful to go to bed at a reasonable hour if one is to rise early to pray. Today, when there are many diversions that can easily distract us from prayer time (e.g., television, radio, films, etc.), one must often renounce some good, interesting alternatives in order to be a faithful pray-er.

2. Mental prayer demands quiet. Naturally, an apostolic community cannot be completely cut off from its contacts with the poor, as is evident in Saint Vincent's conferences to the Daughters of Charity. Nonetheless, one should choose a prayer time when noise and interruptions are un-

likely, when telephones and doorbells will not be ringing. That is one of the reasons why communities have traditionally chosen to pray early in the morning before the busy pace of the day's activities begins. Dietrich Bonhoeffer states: "Silence is nothing else but waiting for God's word."[36]

3. It is important to be acquainted with various methods, by having, so to speak, a "prayer repertory."[37] The four types of prayer described earlier in this article may be useful in this regard. Different methods will be appropriate at different times in life. We may find ourselves, at later stages in life, returning to methods we used earlier.

4. The pray-er needs to be nourished. Some of the principal elements in the diet are the reading of sacred scripture, good spiritual reading, and, especially in an apostolic spirituality, live, reflective contact with Christ in the person of the poor.

5. Prayer should result in renewed self-definition.[38] Through it, our values should become redefined and take on an increasingly evangelical character. Prayer should lead to continued conversion. It should result in acts of charity and justice. This is why Saint Vincent insisted on "practical resolutions."

6. The pray-er should not focus too much on what *he* or *she* says. What God is communicating is more important. In the long run, prayer is a relationship. While words have a privileged place in a relationship, nonetheless communication goes far beyond words. Some of its deepest forms are non-verbal. Those who are deeply in love can often spend significant periods of time together while saying very little. "Mere" presence is a sign of fidelity. Jesus, in fact, warns us against the multiplication of words in prayer (Mt 6:7).[39]

7. Since we are needy, our prayer will often be one of petition, but it is very important that our prayer also take on the other biblical "moods": praise, thanksgiving, wonder, confidence, anguish, abandonment, resignation. Typically Christian prayer is filled with thanksgiving.

8. As Jesus recommends (Mt 6:10), we should often pray to do or accept God's will, however it might manifest itself in our lives. This is

---

36. Bonhoeffer, *Life Together.*
37. Wilkie Au, *By Way of the Heart, Toward a Holistic Christian Spirituality* (Mahwah: Paulist Press, 1989) 92.
38. Margaret Miles, *Practicing Christianity* (New York: Crossroad, 1988) 142.
39. Cf. SV XII, 328, where, in the context of praying the office, Saint Vincent, following Chrysostom, compares mindless rattling of words to the barking of dogs!

what Saint Vincent meant when he recommended indifference as a predisposition for prayer. This is especially important in times of discernment.

9. Since we are human, and therefore embodied, physical and environmental conditions can help or inhibit prayer. Images, candles, incense, the beauty of the setting, a tabernacle, lighting, music—all can be aids to our praying.

10. Distractions are inevitable, since the mind is incapable of focusing on a single object over long periods of time. When distractions are persistent, it is often best to focus on them rather than flee from them, and to make them a topic of our conversation with the Lord.

11. Sharing prayer can be very useful. Each of us has limited insights. We can profit very much from those of others. The faith-witness of others can deepen our own faith. This is surely one of the reasons why Saint Vincent encouraged frequent repetition of prayer. Though that practice became over-stylized in the course of the years, it can find many more flexible forms today.

12. Faithful praying demands perseverance. The search for God is a long journey, in which the prayer climbs mountains, descends into valleys, and sometimes gets stuck on ledges. Saint Vincent encourages the Daughters of Charity by telling them that Saint Teresa spent twenty years without being able to meditate even though she took part faithfully in prayer (SV IX, 424). Sometimes we may feel that we are "wasting time" (SV IX, 50) in prayer, or we may experience long-lasting "dryness" (SV IX, 634), and be tempted to quit. We should resist the temptation. The journey will bring great rewards.

13. The ultimate criterion of prayer is always *life*: "By their fruits you shall know them" (Mt 7:20, 12:33; Lk 6:44). Unfortunately, experience demonstrates that some of those who pray quite regularly may be very difficult to live with. One might, charitably, say that they would perhaps be even worse if they did not pray! But at the same time one might legitimately ask if their prayer has any real connection with life. Ultimately, one cannot judge, in an individual case, what is really going on between God and a person in the depths of his or her being. But one can surely conclude, in general, that there is something very much wrong with prayer that does not result in change of life.

"Let us give ourselves to God," Saint Vincent says repeatedly to the

Vincentians, as well as to the Daughters of Charity.[40] He has deep confidence in God, whom he sees both as father and mother, into whose hands he can place himself and his works.[41] The journal written by Jean Gicquel recounts how Saint Vincent told Frs. Almeras, Berthe, and Gicquel, on June 7, 1660, just four months before his death: "To be consumed for God, to have no goods nor power except for the purpose of consuming them for God. That is what our Savior did himself, who was consumed for love of his Father" (SV XIII, 179).

This great man of action was also a contemplative, caught up in God and consumed by his love. His contemplation of God's love overflowed into practical love for the poor. He encourages his sons and daughters:

> Let us all give ourselves completely to the practice of prayer, since it is by it that all good things come to us. If we persevere in our vocation, it is thanks to prayer. If we succeed in our employments, it is thanks to prayer. If we do not fall into sin, it is thanks to prayer. If we remain in charity and if we are saved, all that happens thanks to God and thanks to prayer. Just as God refuses nothing to prayer, so also he grants almost nothing without prayer. (SV XI, 407)

---

40. For a striking statement of Saint Vincent's attitude before God, cf. SV XII, 133-34, 146-47.
41. SV V, 534; VI, 444; VIII, 55, 256; X, 503.

To the Members
of the
Congregation of the Mission

Some Hopes for the World-Wide Congregation[1]

The prophet Joel tells us that young men will see visions and old men will dream dreams (Jl 3:1).

As brothers in the Congregation, I hope that we can dream the same dreams so that together we can bring them about. Let me share with you some of my hopes for the Congregation over the next several years.

1. *I would like to see the Congregation of the Mission, as a whole, grow to be much more missionary, mobile, flexible, responsive to the needs of the world-wide Church.*

To that end, as you know, I made appeals in October 1992 and 1993 for volunteers for the missions. I was delighted with the response. We have begun new missions in Albania, Tanzania, the Solomon Islands, China, Bolivia, and a new territory in Mozambique. We have also strengthened significantly the Province of Cuba and the Vice-Province of Mozambique.

Next year we hope to focus on the Ukraine and parts of Eastern Europe as well as reinforcing the missions in Tanzania and Bolivia.

I want to say publicly that the confreres have been most generous in their response to my appeal and that the Visitors as a whole have been wonderfully cooperative and supportive.

But this renewed flexibility involves not only the willingness of Confreres to go to new, unknown places. It involves a supple mentality in regard to evangelization itself. Today more than ever we are conscious that lay people have an essential role in announcing the good news.[2] One of the principal tasks of the priests and brothers of the Congregation is to form lay people to participate more fully in the evangelization of the poor (C 1).

---

1. Updated version of a talk to Vincentian confreres at an ongoing formation session in Paris, August 16, 1993.
2. *Christifideles Laici*, 7.

2. *I would like to see all the Confreres of the Congregation engaged actively in on-going Vincentian formation.*

All our recent documents emphasize the need for on-going formation. The Constitutions affirm that formation in the Congregation is a life-long process (C 77). The last four General Assemblies have discussed it at length. The most recent Assembly states that "the Congregation and each Province should be committed to putting in place as soon as possible plans for ongoing formation, which will be paths of conversion that can lead Confreres to deepen their Vincentian charism and vocation and acquire the competency required by new evangelization."[3]

To that end, we have established an International Center for On-going Vincentian Formation in Paris with a team whose members come from various continents.

This project has been greeted with warm enthusiasm not only in Paris, where it has brought about considerable change in the life of the Mother House, but by the Visitors as a whole, whom we consulted about it.

Each year we will sponsor two four-month programs. Two groups of thirty to fifty Confreres will take part in them. We hope to offer a program of integral formation, embracing the various aspects of Vincentian life: our heritage, our spirituality, apostolic life, community life, human development.

3. *I would hope that the Congregation could open several significant works among the clergy.*

We receive many requests, particularly from Africa and Asia. Flexibility is crucial in our response to these requests.

The new mission that we are undertaking in the Solomon Islands involves the opening of a seminary. The mission in Tanzania has possible links with formation in that country too. The appeals that we have received from Russia and China, moreover, are also linked to our involvement in the training of priests.

One of the principal problems we face, however, is that those who have been trained for formation work come, for the most part, from other cultures and speak other languages. Is there sufficient flexibility within

---

3. *Final Document of the 38th General Assembly of the Congregation of the Mission*, New Men, #4, 1992.

the Congregation to make the adaptation that is necessary if we are to respond to the appeals that we receive? I think so, but we will have to work hard at it.

Beyond these appeals from Africa, Asia, and sometimes Latin America, within each culture we must ask ourselves: What are the deepest needs of the clergy today *here* and *now?* Can we Vincentians minister to those needs in some significant way?

4. *I would hope that the Congregation could respond to Pope John Paul's call to us "to search out more than ever, with boldness, humility and skill, the causes of poverty and encourage short- and long-term solutions."* [4]

Some of our provinces, because of their very significant resources, particularly in the universities, can be an effective instrument in responding to that call. For example, St. John's University in New York City has just established a Social Justice Chair.

Along the same lines, I would hope that many individual Confrères would develop an expertise in regard to the social teaching of the Church (S 11 §3) and would develop effective methods of communicating it.

Do the diocesan priests whom we train come to sense that Vincentians are "experts" in the social teaching of the Church, and do they leave our seminaries well prepared to share it with others?

5. *I would hope that the Congregation could develop prayer forms which are "something beautiful for God" and attractive to the young.* What do I mean concretely when I say this?

My experience in several years of visiting the provinces is that our common prayer leaves much to be desired. It is often far from beautiful, far from attractive to young people. On the other hand, I have visited new communities whose prayer is strikingly beautiful and to which young people flock.

In a revision of our prayer, I would envision:

a. a form of morning and evening prayer adapting the structure of the breviary to our own tradition (one could also think of having this approved by the Church, if that seemed advisable)

---

4. John Paul II, Address to the Delegates of the 37th General Assembly, 1986.

* using a modified cycle of psalms that might be grouped around certain themes linked with our tradition and the needs of the universal Church
* using some readings from Saint Vincent
* providing time for meditation and sharing after the readings
* modifying the petitions to focus on some of our Vincentian concerns
* integrating some of our traditional prayers, like the De Profundis and the Expectatio Israel

b. models for sharing our faith and our prayer, as recommended in article 46 of our Constitutions

* meditating on readings from Saint Vincent and then sharing our thoughts, as in *a* above
* meditating on the Sunday readings and preparing the Sunday homily together
* some form of *revision de vie*

c. a compendium of Vincentian hymns, of revised Vincentian prayers

d. suggestions as to ways in which our Vincentian prayer would be open to others

We have named an international committee, which has had two meetings in recent months and is developing a book of prayer for the Congregation.

6. *I would hope that we can develop renewed forms of community living.*

My concern is this: In recent years, it seems to me, we have been able to find a considerable number of renewed, creative ways of serving the poor. But, along with many other Congregations, we have had much difficulty in finding ways of significantly renewing our community living.

Many of the practices and structures that gave shape to community living in an earlier era have disappeared. In the majority of cases, we could surely not now return to those same structures. Most of them served their purpose in their own time, but gradually became over-formalized, inflexible, and out-dated. Still, they often aimed at values that have abiding validity: unity with one another, common vision and energy in the apostolate, prayer, *revision de vie*, penance and conversion.

With the passing away of former practices, we have not yet, unfortunately, come up with sufficient contemporary means for forming "New Communities."

What do I envision might be some elements toward a solution?

One of the principal means that our Constitutions propose for the building up of a living community is the local community plan (C 27). This plan is, in a sense, a covenant entered into by the members of the local community, by which they pledge to work toward certain common goals and engage in certain common practices. It is to include: apostolic activity, prayer, the use of goods, Christian witness where we work, on-going formation, times for group reflection, necessary time for relaxation and study, and an order of day. It is to be evaluated and revised periodically (S 16).

Beyond this legislated structure, our experience too, both in the past and in the present, teaches that some of the means that have been most highly valued in community-building are: communal prayer, faith-sharing, regular meetings, meals together, simplicity in the use of material goods, communal penance, times of relaxing together.

But often the *concrete forms* for revitalizing these means are lacking in local communities. To find or create those forms we need creativity, the ability to listen to each other, and fidelity to the common plans we agree on.

In some ways I find this the most difficult of the challenges to come to grips with.

7. *I would hope that the Congregation will develop active, vital contact with the various Vincentian lay groups and that we will be able to contribute to their formation, as has often been requested of us.*

There are between 1 and 2 million people in our lay groups. That makes for quite a large Vincentian family! There are more than 240,000 members of the A.I.C. (International Association of Charity), the group Saint Vincent called the Ladies of Charity. There are more than 850,000 members of the Vincent de Paul Society in more than 122 countries. Besides that, there are very numerous Vincentian Youth groups. The one in Spain has at least 30,000 members.

Our Constitutions call us to be involved in the formation of the Laity and to assist them toward a fuller participation in the evangelization of the poor (C 1). Are we actively involved with these lay groups? Do we play a significant role in their formation?

8. *I would hope that the Congregation would learn to use the media effectively in its evangelization.*
Is this a vain hope? Maybe. But I think we should give it a try! There are countless documents on the need to use the media in evangelization, catechesis, teaching. Catholics were certainly pioneers in the use of television as a tool for ministry. Most of us remember the days when everybody (Catholic and non-Catholic) was glued to the TV to watch Bishop Sheen.

Since that time, however, we have made little progress. Evangelical groups now certainly outshine us in the use of the media. Even more significantly, those who have values contrary to the Gospel use the media very effectively to communicate their point of view. They consistently communicate the need to have *more*, the need for immediate gratification. They communicate a concept of love that is frequently overly romantic, overly casual, and quite irresponsible.

If we were half as effective in using the media to communicate the values that are most important to us, we would make enormous progress in the new evangelization.

We have named an international committee with members from five continents to suggest ways in which the Congregation can use the media more effectively.

Those are my hopes. Will you join me in making them become a reality?

Toward a New Evangelization Reflections on the Congregation of the Mission[1]

In times of renewal, "young men see visions and old men dream dreams," the prophet Joel tells us (cf. Jl 3:1; also Acts 2:17). Today I ask the Lord to stimulate all of us to new dreams and to new efforts at making them come true.

Toward a New Evangelization

Pope John Paul II has made the expression "new evangelization" part of the contemporary Catholic vocabulary. Few topics have received more attention in the Church in recent years. He speaks of an evangelization that is new in its ardor, in its methods and in its expression.[2]

But John Paul II's teaching has many antecedents over the last several decades. Noteworthy among these is John XXIII's opening address at the Second Vatican Council, where he called for a new expression of the Christian faith:

The substance of the ancient doctrine of the deposit of faith is one thing, and the way in which it is presented is another.[3]

In the same discourse he also stated: "At the same time she [the Church] must ever look to the present, to the new conditions and new forms of life introduced into the modern world which have opened new avenues."[4]

The Medellín document, which had dramatic effects in Latin America,

1. Talk to members of the Eastern Province of the Congregation of the Mission in Philadelphia, June 1993.
2. Discourse at the 19th Ordinary Assembly of CELAM, Haiti, March 9, 1983; also, in the Dominican Republic, October 12, 1984.
3. John XXIII, Opening Address, October 11, 1962, in *The Documents of Vatican II*, edited by Walter Abbot (New York, 1966) 715.
4. *Ibid.*, 714.

called for a re-evangelization of human existence (VIII, 8). It envisioned a Latin American Church that would be an Evangelizer of the Poor, committed to living in solidarity with them (XIV, 8). The final document at Puebla continued this analysis of a renewed evangelization (340f). The Santo Domingo document, building on the experience of two decades, provides an extensive development of the contents of "new evangelization" (Conclusions 23ff).

Almost all commentators agree that Paul IV, while not using the term "new evangelization" is one of its principal architects. *Evangelii Nuntiandi* provides some of the richest source materials for the new evangelization:

> Evangelization loses much of its force and effectiveness if it does not take into consideration the actual people to whom it is addressed, if it does not use their language, their signs and symbols, if it does not answer the questions they ask, and if it does not have an impact on their concrete life. (#63)

Naturally, like many popular expressions, "new evangelization" has taken on a variety of meanings. Also, some controversy has arisen over the terms "new evangelization" or "re-evangelization," the role of the charismatic movement in the process of "new evangelization," the relationship in the past between "evangelization" and "colonization." Leaving aside these controversies for now, today I want to focus on the positive implications of a new evangelization.

Some Reactions

"Nothing is new"

Of course, there are those who, like Qoheleth, feel that nothing is new under the sun (Eccl 1:9). There is a hidden truth in this assertion, but one that needs to be balanced by another truth. The New Testament provides a basis for those holding this position. "Christ is the same yesterday, today, and forever" (Heb 13:8). The fullness of revelation has broken into history in the person of Jesus and the announcement of the reign of God. So, "guard the deposit of faith" (2 Tim 1:14). "If I preach any other gospel, let me be *anathema*" (Gal 1:8).

This fundamental stance emphasizes the *already*, sometimes at the expense of the *not yet*. It accents the basic creed, while being slow to acknowledge that there is development in credal statements.

"Everything is new"

Some are always in process. They are uneasy with the stable, the structured, the given. They are eager for the old things to pass away and for the new to emerge.

There are ample grounds for this position in the New Testament. "If anyone is in Christ, he is a new creation" (2 Cor 5:17). "Behold, all things are new" (2 Cor 5:17). "I will create a new heaven and a new earth" (Is 65:17; cf. Rev 21:1). The good news is *news*.

This fundamental stance emphasizes the *not yet*, sometimes at the expense of the *already*. It accents the Church as mystery, as fathomless, as always revealing the inexhaustible riches of Christ. It cites the many historical instances of development of doctrine. It focuses today on the continually changing interface of Christ and culture.

Of course, the truth lies in a tension between these two views. As Matthew's gospel reminds us: "The wise steward brings forth from his storehouse new things and old" (Mt 13:52).

"What is really new?"

In his discourse given in Santo Domingo on October 12, 1984, Pope John Paul speaks of an evangelization that is new in its:

Ardor

Here the emphasis is on the conversion of the evangelizer. "We have found the Messiah, the Christ," the disciples cry out in John's gospel (1:41). Only someone who knows the Lord and loves him deeply can proclaim the word of God with joy, enthusiasm, conviction.

There are many ways of conversion. The focus in new evangelization is not on any particular path, like that of the charismatic movement, of the neo-catechumenate, or of any new form of community springing up in the Church, though many are in fact converted in and through new communities. One must surely be converted. Finding the way is the challenge.

In this light, the new evangelization raises a series of questions for us. Have I really found a way of conversion myself? Has the Congregation as a whole been genuinely converted? Has live contact with the poor been for us, as it was for Saint Vincent, the path to conversion? Have the poor revealed to us how God sees the world's priorities?

Methods

There are many new means at hand. They too pose enormously challenging questions to us.

Do many in the Church, or the Congregation, really use the mass media (TV, radio, movies, the press) as a means for evangelizing? Are there many provinces that have trained even one person in the use of the media and have organized one good media project? Do many in the Congregation use computers to full advantage in pastoral activities?

In our pastoral methodology, do we work not only *for* the poor, but *with* them? Do we regard base communities as a peculiar Latin American thing, or do we work at forming Christian communities wherever we evangelize?

Expression

Every era and every place has its own language and culture or, better, its own languages and cultures. Today, differences in culture pose an increasing challenge, since we live in an information society, where rapid communication brings us into contact with the global community.

In the Church, we live in an ecumenical era. In philosophy and theology, hermeneutics play a very significant role. There is strong emphasis on the need for the inculturation of theology.

In fact, in contemporary Church documents, there are some accents that are quite new. Not that they have never existed before; you can find most of them, at least in some form, in the Fathers of the Church. But as the Church interfaces with contemporary societies and cultures, there is a new emphasis on:

— the preferential option for the poor
— the effects of sin on social structures
— the systemic aspects of justice and injustice
— life issues (war, peace-making, abortion, euthanasia,
       capital punishment)
— the erosion of family structures and sexual morality
— integral liberation
— ecology.

Beyond these new emphases in Church documents and contemporary theology, one can also discern in our 1984 Constitutions and in the official documents of the Congregation in recent years a number of significantly new accents:

— on Christ as the Evangelizer of the Poor
— on the link between evangelization and action for justice
— on searching out the causes of poverty and concrete solutions
— on specializing in the Church's social teaching
— on investigating the new forms of poverty
— on being evangelized by the poor
— on the poor as not merely the object of evangelization, but its subject
— on forming basic Christian communities
— on a global world-view.

A Description of Evangelization and Some Critical Distinctions

As a basis for the reflections that follow, I offer you this description of evangelization used by Paul VI in *Evangelii Nuntiandi*:

> Evangelization is a complex process made up of varied elements: the renewal of humanity, witness, explicit proclamation, inner adherence, entry into the community, acceptance of signs, apostolic initiative. These elements may appear to be contradictory, indeed mutually exclusive. In fact they are complementary and mutually enriching. Each one must always be seen in relationship with the others. (#24)

From the writings of Paul VI and John Paul II, it is evident that evangelization has many facets, all of which play a significant role in the overall picture. Within that context, let me highlight two critical distinctions that play a significant role in describing evangelization in the Vincentian tradition:

Evangelizing "by word and work"; serving "spiritually and corporally"

Saint Vincent was deeply convinced of the link between what we say and what we do. Again and again, therefore, he spoke of evangelization by "word and work." He calls both the Vincentians and Daughters of Charity to serve the poor "spiritually and corporally." When speaking to the members of the Congregation, he warned us:

> If there are any among us who think they are in the Congregation of the Mission to preach the gospel to the poor but not to comfort them, to supply their spiritual but not their temporal wants, I reply that we ought to assist them and have them assisted in every way, by ourselves and by others. . . . To do this is to preach the gospel by words and by works. (SV XII, 87)

He tells the Daughters of Charity again and again that their works must be accompanied by words of faith.[5]

First, do; then, teach. That is Saint Vincent's rule for "effective" evangelization. In other words, Saint Vincent sees preaching and human promotion as complementary to one another, and as integral to the evangelization process.

Direct and indirect evangelization

Neither Saint Vincent nor the history of the Congregation provide any grounds for a fundamentalism in regard to evangelization of the poor. Saint Vincent clearly recognized that not all could serve the poor directly and that some would necessarily serve them indirectly. He handled this dispute in his own lifetime. As examples, he cites seminary teachers and directors of the Daughters of Charity. He saw their role as necessary if the poor were to be served well. There will always be similar cases.

There is a need for caution in using the direct/indirect distinction. It must be evoked with great moderation. Unless a very large number of our members is involved in direct evangelization we will hardly merit the name "missionaries."

---

5. SV IX, 59; IX, 593; XI, 364; XI, 592.

Toward a New Evangelization in the Congregation of the Mission

Our most recent General Assembly calls the Congregation to make six commitments:

1. *Remembering that Saint Vincent's encounter with the poor was a decisive factor in his life, we will have personal contact with people whom our society has disinherited and abandoned.*

This is the peculiarly Vincentian way of conversion. It is not the only one, of course. But it is the way that Saint Vincent trod and the way in which he calls the Company to walk. If the new evangelization is one that is to be new in its ardor, then it must rest upon the foundation of a genuine conversion.

Let me simply add here that the controlling *spiritual* force that will enable us to live out this first commitment of the General Assembly is the lived conviction that we who are Vincentians follow Christ *as the Evangelizer of the Poor.* Focus on, and commitment to, *this* Christ is the heart of Vincentian spirituality.

Is it really possible for everyone to have first-hand contact with the poor? Certainly not everyone can have as his principal ministry one which brings him into direct contact with the poor. The Superior General is one example of this. But I would suggest that for most of us it is possible to have at least *some* direct contact, even if not every day.

2. *Recognizing the complexity of our world today, we will investigate and urge others to study the root causes of poverty in order "to promote long- and short-term solutions, which are concrete, flexible and efficacious."*[6]

The direct/indirect distinction comes into play here. Does one do more good by ministering directly to the hungry person, giving him food, or by investigating the causes of famine and working toward a resolution of the problem? The pope calls on us as Vincentians to use our gifts not only in direct service to the poor, but also in the kind of indirect service that will be even more beneficial in the long run.

The Congregation can play a very significant role here. We have

6. Address of John Paul II to the delegates at the General Assembly of 1986.

formidable educational and financial resources for investigating the causes of poverty. Recently, I met with the presidents of three of our Vincentian-sponsored universities to encourage them to mobilize the energies of their faculties, staff, and students to study the root causes of poverty and search for solutions.

In our preaching, we can also encourage others to develop a global world-view, and challenge them to make their own an ethic in which justice is a foundation stone.

Are there ways in which we can engage in a critique of contemporary society from the point of view of justice? Anyone living in Italy, as I do, is very conscious today of the need to evangelize economic and political life, since gospel values and ethical values have given way to wholesale corruption. The same is true in many countries.

This kind of critical, prophetic role of the Church and of theology creates a new relationship between the Church and the world, not one of alliance with the powerful, but one of solidarity with the oppressed and defense of the rights of the poor.

3. *We will give a privileged place in our own formation and in the formation of priests and laity to a spirit of dialogue and collaboration with contemporary society, in the light of the social teaching of the Church. The goal will be to promote creative solidarity in favor of the poor, who long for their own liberation and personal well-being.*

I want to make three points in this regard:

a. The General Assembly speaks of dialogue with contemporary society. I hereby appeal to all candidates for the Congregation, and as many members as possible, to become bilingual. Dialogue and mobility in contemporary society demand it. In the United States, for example, almost fifty percent of the Catholics do not speak English as their first language. Spanish has become an essential tool for a missionary there.

Saint Vincent felt strongly about the need to learn other languages. He told the confreres:

> Now the diversity of languages is very great, not only in Europe, Africa and Asia, but also in Canada. For we see by the reports of the Jesuit Fathers that there are as many languages as there are tribes. The Hurons do not speak like the Iroquois, nor the latter like their neighbors. And a person who

understands one group of Indians does not understand the others.

How then can Missionaries, bearing these differences of language in mind, go throughout the world announcing the Gospel if they know only their own language? (SV XII, 26-27)

b. The statement also speaks of the social teaching of the Church. Are there ways in which not just our educational institutions, but all of us, can communicate the Church's social doctrine more effectively. Pope John Paul II writes very forcefully in *Centesimus Annus*: "The 'new evangelization' which the modern world urgently needs and which I have emphasized many times, must include among its essential elements *a proclamation of the Church's social doctrine*" (#5). The Church has been proclaiming this doctrine in a rather clear way now for more than one hundred years. Are Catholics really well evangelized in this regard? Is this social doctrine part of their explicit consciousness? Are we Vincentians "experts" in teaching this social doctrine?

c. Do the clergy and laity in whose formation we assist really become "experts" in the Church's social doctrine? Do they look back on their Vincentian teachers and directors with gratitude for having moved them to drink deeply from this rich source?

4. *We will give to all our pastoral activity a clear missionary character, attending to the most abandoned and marginated and fostering the effective participation of everyone in the life of the Christian community. We will be ready to hand our work over to others when we consider our mission completed.*

The key here is mobility. The missionary's goal is the formation of new or renewed local communities. He is aware that there are "other villages where the gospel must be preached" (cf. Mk 1:38) and that therefore his time commitment in a given place is limited. When the Christian community is self-sufficient, the missionary moves on.

The statement speaks of the effective participation of everyone in the life of the Christian community. Today we are aware that the poor are not just the *object* of evangelization, but its *subject*. The poor themselves evangelize. Our evangelization is *with* and *for* them.

Consequently, the new evangelization calls for a new way of being for the missionary. His ministry is characterized by community-building, by the active participation of all, by the distribution of functions, by the emergence of new ministries and charisms, by solidarity with the oppressed.[7] I must raise a question here that pertains to Vincentians in many parts of the world. There are now hundreds of thousands of basic Christian communities throughout the world. More and more in these communities, the gospel is read together and meditated on, interpreted in an environment of prayer and communal sharing, and lived in relationship to the problems within the people's culture. Has this mode of evangelization been sufficiently explored and put into practice in the Congregation?

What is being described here, in the second, third, and fourth commitments cited above, is a very demanding pastoral methodology, which had already been outlined in the 1990 document "Visitors in Service of the Mission" (p. 16):

* to work within the world of the poor (the poor as a class), not just with isolated persons (Lines of Action 1986, 4 and 11);

* to work on the level of structures, not just in responding to particular situations (Lines of Action 1986, 6 and 11);

* to work to confront injustice, not just to meet the needs of individual poor people (Lines of Action 1986, 4 and 11);

* to work with groups (small communities), so that the poor person is an agent, and not simply an object, of evangelization (Lines of Action 1986, 4 and 11).

5. *We will foster the work of the popular missions and the missions ad gentes, working for the creation, the growth and the maturity of Christian communities, which will be both evangelized and evangelizing and which will promote the integral development of persons.* *Centesimus Annus* puts the challenge very clearly:

> Present circumstances are leading to a reaffirmation of the positive value of an authentic theology of integral human liberation. (#26)

---

7. Leonardo Boff, *Nova Evangelização. Perspectiva dos Oprimidos* (Fortaleza: Vozes, 1990) 122-26. In this very interesting work, the author also mentions new *contents* in the new evangelization: a new kind of spirituality, a new relationship of the Church with the world. In regard to *method*, he focuses especially on the poor as the *subject* of evangelization.

Integral development and integral liberation are two key phrases in our own documents and in those of Pope John Paul II. Integral human liberation embraces all the aspects of people's lives: personal, social, intellectual, affective, cultural, religious.

Renewed popular missions and missions *ad gentes* will develop new methods for fostering integral liberation, a new pedagogy that is adapted to the oppressed,[8] where the educator and those being educated learn mutually, where we not only evangelize but are evangelized by the poor.

As in Jesus' ministry, so also in the new evangelization there will also be new recipients of evangelization: the culture, popular religiosity, marginalized women, prostitutes, street people, AIDS victims, those without housing.

6. *Our Congregation commits itself in Eastern Europe to at least one missionary project as a concrete sign of our community's participation in new evangelization.*

As you know, we sent three missionaries to Albania last year and two more this year (there are also three groups of Daughters of Charity). Although one hears less of Albania, it is probably the poorest country in all of Europe. Nothing functions and nothing is available. The economic and political structure of the country was utterly devastated during the years of communist domination.

We now also have missionaries working in the Ukraine, in Byelorussia, and Lithuania. We hope to send more.

Let me conclude by asking these fundamental questions. Can the Church, as it commits itself to a new evangelization, really become a Church of the poor, as Pope John XXIII called it to be in his opening address at Vatican II? Will we, the members of the Congregation of the Mission, really be followers of Christ *as the Evangelizer of the Poor*, as our Constitutions call us to be? Will our provinces really be communities of priests and brothers evangelizing the poor and leading others to evangelize them, as their apostolic plans envision? The answer can surely be *yes* to all these questions.

---

8. Cf. Paulo Freire, *Pedagogy of the Oppressed* (New York: Herder and Herder, 1970).

On Being a Missionary Today[1]

I ask you today, my brothers, to join me in reflecting on our name. We are members of the Congregation of the *Mission*. Saint Vincent reminds us that people from the earliest times, spontaneously called us "the *missionaries*" (cf. SV III, 356). The Lord sends us out. Our vocation is not to remain fixed in a single place, to sink permanent roots. Jesus speaks to us as he did to his disciples at the end of Mark's gospel: "Go! Go into the whole world and preach the gospel to every creature" (Mk 16:15).

Mission is not merely an activity of the Church; it is its very being. Over the course of history the Church has used different images of mission.[2] If one thinks of the "reign of God" as the New Testament fundamental image describing God's advent in the world through the person of Jesus, then "mission" is the image used to describe the Church's role in spreading that reign.[3] As an image, "mission" has had different resonances in different eras.

Mission as *crusade* looks at the world as divided between good and evil, true and false. There is an atmosphere of conquest. In the best of times the conquest is primarily spiritual, but sometimes it has been quite mixed up with economic, political, and cultural power.

Mission as *teaching* focuses on faith as a creed or a body of truths that is to be communicated. There is a stress on knowledge and the use of preaching, teaching, writing, and the media for the communication of revealed truth.

Mission as a *call to conversion* stresses the need for personal change of heart. Each individual is called to be born again in response to a personal and moral challenge. Conversion is seen as a profound personal experience.

Mission as *liberation* aims at the transformation of life starting here

---

1. Talk to participants of the Vincentian Ongoing Formation Center in Paris, September 22, 1994.
2. For much of the analysis of images of mission, I am deeply indebted to M. Amaladoss, "Religious in Mission," a conference given at the International Congress of the Union of Superiors General, Rome, November 22-27, 1993.
3. S. Schneiders, *The Revelatory Text* (San Francisco: Harper, 1991) 32.

and now, though it is not limited to the present. It promotes healing, development, and justice, as the reign of God comes to be realized.

Mission as *witness* focuses on Christian life as a silent but active presence in the midst of a hostile world. The Church lives as a leaven in the diaspora. The minister builds up model communities of service and fellowship.

Mission as *inculturation* evokes the need for Christianity to become incarnate in a particular culture. The gospel interfaces with local cultural, purifying it and at the same time incorporating its riches, maintaining a unity of meaning within a plurality of expressions.

Mission as *dialogue* recognizes other religions as positive elements in God's saving plan. One sees in them the hidden or preparatory activity of the Spirit. The Church in that context is seen as fulfillment, explicitation, or sacramental fullness.

Mission as *pilgrimage* envisions walking with God and with others in the fulfillment of God's plan for the universe, where God's action is mixed up with human imperfection and sinfulness. It envisions the Church as existing for the world, called to animate a movement of peoples toward the realization of God's reign, which is both historical and eschatological.

Mission as *prophecy* radicalizes the proclamation of the good news as it confronts the deficiencies of human cultures and oppressive structures. It seeks to transform culture, to be critical of the easy legitimations of religion, and to challenge the oppressive economico-political and socio-cultural structures.

All of these images tell us something about mission. They all have their strengths and weaknesses. Each has time-conditioned elements. Each contains an abiding truth. While some (e.g., the image of *crusade*) are much more time-conditioned than others, we can learn from them all. In fact, each provides abundant material for meditation.

What then does it mean to be a missionary today? This is a crucial question for us, since it touches on our identity. There is no doubt about our calling: we are members of the Congregation of the *Mission*.

Some Characteristics of Missionaries Today

Let me simply outline for you *some* characteristics of a missionary today. There are surely many others. I encourage you to supplement the list with your own reflections.

An international perspective, a global world view

Three signs, especially, will witness to global awareness in the Congregation.

A first, concrete sign of this awareness is the ability to respond to urgent needs throughout the world. Do not let provincial ties and provincial needs hold you back. When the needs of the Church are greater elsewhere, go with liberty.

A second sign of an international perspective in the Congregation is solidarity among the provinces. I urge you to cooperate with one another. This is already taking place through national and regional meetings of Visitors, but I especially want to encourage you to cooperate in regard to the formation of candidates and in regard to assistance to poorer provinces. There are some things that we can do much better together than separately. Moreover, those of us who are better off materially can surely be of great assistance to those who have less.

Thirdly, a healthy sign of global awareness in the Congregation will be the presence in the General Curia and on our various commissions of confreres of various races and from all continents. An international Congregation needs ties between the center and the provinces. As the provinces of the "Third Church" continue to grow, good communication with the center will be an utter necessity.

Mobility and spreading of the good news

The Church exists to evangelize, to proclaim that Jesus is Lord. So too does the Congregation. This means that the members of the Congregation will be agile, quick to move when new needs arise. Our love will be expansive, like a fire. We will want to tell others the good news that Jesus is alive and present.

I pose this question: Could every province of the Congregation of the Mission take on the responsibility for a mission outside its own territory? In addition, could the Congregation become more missionary not just territorially, but in the heart and will of its members, showing great flexibility in moving to wherever the needs of the poor cry out, both within one's province and outside?

One of the signs that the Congregation is filled with a mobile missionary spirit will be the willingness to relinquish works that are firmly established, and which others can carry on, in order to free confreres for more pressing needs that others are unwilling or unable to meet.

Flexibility

The accent here is on a supple mentality in regard to evangelization. In a time of rapid change, rigidity is an enemy and flexibility an ally. For example, one of the most significant changes that has taken place in the Church since Vatican II is in the role of the laity. Today we are conscious more than ever that lay people have an essential role in announcing the good news.[4] It is for that reason that our Constitutions call the priests and brothers of the Congregation not only to evangelize the poor as missionaries, but to form others—priests, brothers, sisters, lay men and women—to participate more fully in the evangelization of the poor (C 1). Are we flexible in accepting the important roles of lay men and women in evangelizing? Do we have the suppleness to co-operate harmoniously with them?

A greater pluralism in theological perspective and a greater variety in the plans for local community living also demand a flexible mentality. It is crucial that we have the flexibility to live and work with people of differing theological perspectives. In dialoguing and deciding about our local community plans, moreover, much give-and-take is essential.

Foreign languages

Saint Vincent asked, "How can missionaries go throughout the world announcing the Gospel if they know only their own language?" (SV XII, 26-27)

We are an international congregation. We labor in more than seventy countries. Missionary mobility demands that as many of our members as possible be bilingual.

Inculturation

There is always the danger that the ideas, the customs, even the building styles of one world will simply be transported to another. Our great missionaries, like Justin de Jacobis, recognized from the start that

---

4. *Christifideles Laici*, 7.

this is insufficient. The gospel must take root and blossom within the deepest values of each culture. At the same time, it must transform what is not of God within a culture and what violates the human person. Karl Rahner points out that the *globalization* of theology is one of the greatest needs of the Church in the years ahead. He notes that up to the present there has been an unfortunate tendency to "canonize" what was really only a manifestation of the thought patterns of western culture.[5] Right now, many younger and growing provinces, and particularly those responsible for formation within them, face the difficult challenge of teaching philosophy and theology (so often formulated in a European context), while searching for new categories in an African, Asian or South American setting. Similarly, they search for the appropriate forms of expressing poverty, chastity, obedience, and life-long commitment to the poor within cultures very different not only from Saint Vincent's, but also from those of the writers of most of the philosophy, theology, and spiritual reading books written up until recent times. In our service to the diocesan clergy, and in the formation of our own candidates, are we finding the means to present a truly inculturated theology and spirituality?

Along these same lines, the place of women in society and the social mores in relating to them vary greatly from North to South and, in both hemispheres, from continent to continent. To talk with a woman on the street may be as "natural" in Los Angeles as it is "scandalous" in the Islamic Republic of Mauritania. The missionary must know the difference.

Listening for calls

A missionary seeks not his own will but the will of Him who sends him. He is ready to respond to the needs of his religious community and God's people. The calls of God's people are very important. Our own gifts and talents are too. Most modern religious communities attempt to fit calls to the gifts and talents of their individual members. In this context, it is important for every member of the Congregation to let himself be challenged. We must listen well, especially when we are tempted to seek our own security, to remain where we are. Often, responses to challenging calls draw forth from us resources whose existence we never dreamed of;

---

5. Cf. Citation in W. Bühlmann, *The Church of the Future* (Maryknoll: Orbis, 1986) 193.

not only do we serve those who are crying out for help, but we also find ourselves growing in the process.

Continuous formation

The Congregation must continue to emphasize, and find creative means for, integral formation on both initial and ongoing levels. Such integral formation has various aspects: human, spiritual, apostolic, Vincentian, biblical, theological, professional. On all levels, the person himself would be seen as the one primarily responsible for his own formation.

I encourage the provinces to be especially attentive to the formation of confreres in the early years *after* vows or ordination. Bring them together often to share their experiences. Offer them wise mentors. Help them build a deep spiritual foundation, a rootedness in God. It is only in this way that they will be fully alive and persevering in the evangelization of the poor.

Creativity in defining missionary work

Saint Vincent tells us: "Love is inventive to the point of infinity" (SV XI, 146). Over the years, I have admired many confreres for their inventiveness. Because they live in daily contact with the poor they are among the first to know their real needs. It will not be I, who am sitting behind a desk or visiting the provinces. It will not be sociologists or economists, who study the needs of the poor by examining the data they receive. The confreres who are front-line workers will know ahead of us, because the poor will tell them directly. I want to encourage all our missionaries to be inventive in the service of the needs that you discover. Pose the question individually and as a local community: What is this poor person asking of me concretely? What is the deepest need of the person listening to my homily? What is the refugee in a camp in Africa asking? What is the sick person in his or her home crying out for? What is the AIDS patient's acutest pain? Then be creative in ministering to their needs.

For a variety of reasons, particularly the shortage of vocations, in some countries our service in seminaries has been significantly reduced. An important challenge that lies before us as Vincentians is to find other creative means of assisting in the formation of the diocesan clergy in those circumstances.

Expertise in the social teaching of the Church

Pope John Paul II writes very forcefully in *Centesimus Annus:* "The 'new evangelization,' which the modern world urgently needs and which I have emphasized many times, must include among its essential elements *a proclamation of the Church's social doctrine*" (#5). The Church has been proclaiming this doctrine in a rather clear way now for more than one hundred years. Are Catholics really well evangelized in this regard? Is this social doctrine part of their explicit consciousness? I ask all Vincentians to become "experts" in teaching this social doctrine. As followers of Christ, the Evangelizer of the Poor, we must proclaim this aspect of the reign of God by our words and by our works. We must hold up before others the Church's rich teaching, its vision of a kingdom of justice, its denunciation of unjust social structures, its proclamation that the poor must, in every era, occupy a central place in the consciousness of Christians. In our formation work, with both clergy and laity, we must present this social teaching with both clarity and urgency.

Our mission will be truly prophetic today if we preach and teach the Church's social doctrine clearly. And like many prophets, we may perhaps suffer as we do so.

Being a man of God

Witness speaks more eloquently than words. Our lives inevitably say much more than our sermons.

For Vincent de Paul, there is only one driving force: the person of Jesus Christ. "Jesus Christ is the rule of the Mission" (SV XII, 130),[6] he tells the members of the Congregation of the Mission, the center of their life and activity. "Remember, Father," he writes to Monsieur Portail, one of the original members of the Congregation, "that we live in Jesus Christ by the death of Jesus Christ, and that we ought to die in Jesus Christ by the life of Jesus Christ, and that our life ought to be hidden in Jesus Christ and full of Jesus Christ, and that in order to die like Jesus Christ it is necessary to live like Jesus Christ" (SV I, 295).

Vincent warns his followers that they will find true freedom only when Christ takes hold of them. He writes to Antoine Durand, the newly

---

6. Cf. also XI, 53: "Let us walk with assurance on the royal road on which Jesus Christ will be our guide and leader."

appointed superior of the seminary at Agde: "It is therefore essential for you, Father, to empty yourself in order to put on Jesus Christ" (SV XI, 343-44).

We fulfill our mission only if we follow Christ as the Evangelizer of the Poor and put on his spirit (C 1), if, as our Constitutions put it, we are holy.

Today, as in every era, the Church needs saints. It needs missionaries who are simple, humble, gentle, self-sacrificing, and filled with effective love. It needs preachers who radiate God's presence. The great missionary is not so much a man whose words are beautiful as a man whose life is striking.

Let me state it very clearly: the missionary today must be holy. Unless he is a man of God, he will not be genuinely effective, nor is he likely to persevere.

It is not the loss of numbers that the Congregation must fear (in fact, our numbers are reasonably stable). It is not the loss of institutions. What we must really fear is the loss of fire in our hearts. What burns in the heart of the true missionary is a deep yearning, a longing to follow Christ as the Evangelizer of the Poor. The genuinely holy missionary *presences* Christ's love. Others sense it in him. He could not hide it even if he wanted to.

To be a *missionary*—that is our calling. Breathe deeply, my brothers, of the missionary spirit that Saint Vincent inspired in the Congregation. Let it fill your minds and hearts. Then, go. "Go into the whole world and preach the gospel to every creature" (Mk 16:15).

Vincentian Formation
in an African Context[1]

My brothers, it is good that we are here. This is the first such meeting, on African soil, in the history of the Congregation. It is a sign of how important Africa has become in the life and the mission of the Company.

Some Factors Influencing What We Say and Do

Our context is very important. Saint Vincent loved Africa. He himself sent the first Missionaries here. But this huge continent is quite different in our day from the Africa he knew. Let me mention three factors that profoundly influence what we say and do today.

The shift from the North to the South

During the fifteen-year pontificate of Paul VI, a striking shift took place in the Church's statistical center of gravity. Striking though it was, few actually noticed it. The turning point arrived in 1970: fifty-one percent of the Catholic population was living in the southern continents. By the year 2000, seventy percent of all Catholics will be in the southern hemisphere.[2] Walbert Bühlmann calls this the "coming of the third Church."[3]

In an existential sense, Catholicism is becoming truly a "world-church," as Karl Rahner pointed out on many occasions.[4]

Many religious communities are experiencing this dramatically. In our own Congregation, for example, while there are few vocations in western

---

1. Opening discourse at the Conference of Visitors of Africa and Madagascar in Kinshasa, June 24, 1994.
2. W. Bühlmann, *The Church of the Future* 4-5.
3. Cf. W. Bühlmann, *The Coming of the Third Church* (Slough, England: St. Paul Publications, 1976).
4. K. Rahner, "The Abiding Significance of the Second Vatican Council," in *Theological Investigations* XX, 90-102; cf. also "The Future of the Church and the Church of the Future," in *Theological Investigations* XX, 103-14.

Europe and North America, where formerly they flourished, the Company is growing not only in Poland, but also in Ethiopia, Eritrea, Nigeria, Zaire, Mozambique, Madagascar, the Philippines, India, Indonesia, Colombia, Mexico, and Central America.

For the Congregation, the opportunities and the challenges are enormous. The confreres from these countries enrich the Congregation with their own cultures and religious traditions. They often, for example, bring us an experience of life lived out continually in intimate contact with the poor. Such provinces frequently have active, even thriving, programs for ministerial formation among both the clergy and the laity. But they also express two striking needs: 1) the need for trained personnel to carry on the work of our own formation; 2) the need for further inculturation of the gospel, so that the Christianity and culture might interact with one another at a deeper level, both enriching and purifying each other. Rahner points out that the *globalization* of theology is one of the greatest needs of the Church in the years ahead. He notes that up to the present there has been an unfortunate tendency to "canonize" what was really only a manifestation of the thought patterns of western culture.[5]

First Synod of Bishops for Africa, Madagascar and the Islands

The Church has just celebrated the first special Synod of Bishops for Africa, Madagascar and the Islands. Its focus was on "The Church in Africa and her evangelizing mission toward the year 2000: 'You will be my witnesses' (Acts 1:8)," under five subheadings: proclamation, inculturation, dialogue, justice and peace, and means of social communication. It treated the inculturation of faith, women's roles and status, and dialogue with other churches, with Islam, and with traditional religions. It examined the roles of priests, religious, laity, families, African theologians, catechists, and others. Both the meeting itself and the lively participation of African representatives are a vivid sign of how deeply the Spirit of the Lord breathes on this continent.

The synod sounded an eloquent call to communion and inculturation: "It is the Church as family which manifests to the world the Spirit which the Son sent from the Father so that there should be communion among all. Jesus Christ, the only begotten and beloved Son, has come to save

---

5. Cf. citation in Bühlmann, *The Church of the Future* 193.

every people and every individual human being. He has come to meet each person in the cultural path inherited from the ancestors. He travels with each person to throw light on his traditions and customs and to reveal to him that these are a prefiguration, distant but certain, of him, the new Adam, the elder of a multitude of brothers, which we are."[6] Our purpose here is not to examine the conclusions of the synod in detail, though this will surely be one of the most important future agenda items for all of our provinces and missions here in Africa.

The pains of turmoil and violence

I cannot leave unmentioned today the pain that the world, the Church, and our own Vincentian family is experiencing here on this continent so rich in faith and varied cultures. Our own Vincentian Family shares in this pain and has suffered from violence, recently in Rwanda and Sierra Leone, and over the years in Burundi, Cameroon, Mozambique, Eritrea, Ethiopia, Nigeria, and Zaire. But these are only the most dramatic examples. Overt or hidden structural violence ravages Africa. The synod reminded us that the Lord has given us two great gifts of the kingdom, which he is in person. These are justice and peace. It demanded greater justice between North and South. It called for an end to presenting Africa "in a ridiculous and insignificant light on the world scene after having brought about and maintained a structural inequality and while upholding unjust terms of trade!"[7] It remembered the dozens of millions of refugees and displaced persons in Rwanda, Sudan, Mozambique, Angola, Liberia, Sierra Leone, Somalia, and parts of Central Africa, and it called upon the United Nations to intervene in order to reestablish peace. It pleaded for a stop to arms sale or the flow of the instruments of violence from the northern hemisphere to the southern. It asked for a substantial, if not total, remission of the continent's debt. At the same time the synod encouraged the churches of Africa to examine their own conscience on the question of financial self-reliance and urged them to do everything to bring this about, particularly through transparent management and a simple lifestyle consonant with the poverty, even misery, of many of Africa's own people.[8]

---

6. *Origins*, vol. 24, n. 1 (May 19, 1994) 5.
7. *Ibid.*, 7.
8. *Ibid.*, 8.

Formation in Africa

Our own meeting focuses on formation in Africa, a topic that the synod too treated. The synod emphasizes several key elements in regard to formation:

1. It envisions the integral formation of people who are well-inserted in their milieu, and who witness therein to the kingdom which is to come.[9]

2. It states that this is to be done by means of evangelization and inculturation, of dialogue and involvement in justice and peace, as well as by means of a presence in the new culture constituted by the world of the mass media.[10]

3. It declares that programs and houses of formation, especially seminaries and novitiates, should reflect the concern manifested by the synod to see inculturation and the social teaching of the Church taken very seriously.[11]

4. It thanks God for the gift of vocations which are increasing everywhere in Africa but calls upon the Church in Africa to receive this gift with responsibility, being concerned with the quality of vocations, the discernment process in identifying them, and the setting up of criteria for admission, and the offering of a rich formation.[12]

5. It calls upon the Church to prepare formators well.[13]

6. It tells formators: "On the quality of your life and on your fidelity to your commitments depends the credibility of what you are teaching the seminarians and the success of the formation that you are giving them. If your intellectual competence is not put at the service of a holy life, you will be increasing in the Church the number of priest functionaries who will not give to the world the only reality that the world expects from them: God."[14] Formators should be genuinely holy—role models for our students.

7. It tells religious: "You will succeed in inculturating religious life in Africa only by assuming, as it were, by representation and anticipation, the profound values that make up the life of our cultures and express the

---

9. "Final Message of the Synod for Africa," *Origins*, vol. 24, n. 1 (May 19, 1994) § 49.
10. *Ibid.*
11. *Ibid.*, § 50.
12. *Ibid.*, § 51.
13. *Ibid.*, § 51.
14. *Ibid.*, § 52.

end pursued by our peoples. In this way you will give spiritual hospitality to Christ, chaste, poor and obedient, who has come not to destroy but to fulfill."[15]

8. It tells seminarians: "Be convinced that spiritual formation is the key to the whole of your formation. An intense prayer life and a generous spiritual combat will enable you to properly discern your vocation and to grow as witnesses. . . ."[16] It encourages them to strive after the simple lifestyle of laborers for the gospel in solidarity with the poor of the continent.[17]

Vincentian Formation in Africa and Madagascar

What should seminary formation be like in Africa when the gospel and the Church are truly to be inculturated here? There is always the danger that the buildings and the ideas of another world will be simply transported to Africa. Our great missionaries, like Justin de Jacobis, recognized from the start that this is insufficient. The gospel must take root and blossom within the deepest values of African cultures. At the same time it must transform what is not of God and what violates the human person.

In each African country, there is a need for communion with the larger worldwide Vincentian family and, at the same time, genuine rootedness of the Congregation within Africa. Toward that end, formation is crucial.

Let me place before you a series of challenges, while being very conscious that you have already generously begun to labor at them.

1. I ask you, in dialogue with one another, to make *real* for our seminarians the five Vincentian virtues. We know what these virtues meant for Saint Vincent. There are many studies in that regard. What do they mean in an African context?

a. Simplicity involves communicating the truth as it is, without dissimulation. How can one best express here the core of Jesus' statement that our yes should mean yes and our no, no (Mt 5:37)? How can simplicity be expressed here? How do the relationships of the speaker and the listener (superiors, elders, the young) affect communication?

15. *Ibid.*, § 58.
16. *Ibid.*, § 60 and 61.
17. *Ibid.*, § 61.

b. *Humility* for Saint Vincent involves a grateful recognition that all is gift. It involves a consciousness that we are God's creatures, that we depend on him, upon one another, and upon the created reality around us. It involves an awareness that we are sinners too and that we need God's forgiveness. How will this consciousness be expressed in the African context? What concrete forms will humility take?

c. *Meekness* entails gentleness, warmth in relating, non-violence. The Church has surely had little success in proclaiming that "the meek shall possess the land" (Mt 5:5) in Europe, Asia, and the Americas, as well as in Africa. What can be done to remedy this for the future? What can African formation do to wipe out strife, especially violence, for instance, between tribes?

d. *Mortification* involves renunciation of certain goods in order to pursue other more important ones which we have freely chosen. It involves disciplined labor in the service of the gospel. It involves the sacrifices necessary for keeping our commitments. What concrete forms should mortification take in Africa? What are the concrete areas in which seminarians should learn to become disciplined men?

e. *Zeal* is love that is on fire. It involves burning love for the person of the Lord and a "new ardor" for a "new evangelization." It implies hard work, the attitude of a servant. Its enemies, Saint Vincent tells us, are sloth and indiscreet zeal. What forms do zeal and its enemies take in Africa at the dawn of a new millennium?

2. What is the concrete meaning of the Vincentian vows in Africa today?

a. What are the challenges for living out the vow of *poverty?* How should it be lived out concretely in societies where families may make increasing demands on their sons, as they become better educated and take on a prestigious societal role? What constitutes a simple lifestyle in this context? How can we live in greater solidarity with the poor?

b. *Celibacy* has its own particular challenges in Africa. Africa is not alone in this regard. Celibacy is difficult. Each culture in each part of the world has experienced struggles and trials as it labored to find the ways of living out this gospel value genuinely and with great simplicity. What are the obstacles to celibacy in each country? How should it be lived out concretely in a context where generativity is held in such high esteem?

c. How does one live out dialogue and obedience concretely in a context where authority structures have been traditionally different from those in other parts of the world? Where wisdom figures, like elders, play a very significant role? How can candidates be formed to express their views directly to superiors?

d. Saint Vincent regarded *stability* as a keystone in the life of the Congregation and as crucial for the service of the poor. What are the values within African society that support it? What are those that work against it?

3. Tribal structures, which play a very significant role in African societies, have the potential for mutual enrichment or for profound division. How will our formation programs help our candidates to recognize the richness of their various heritages, and those of others, while at the same time living out profoundly the deeper, more universal bonds that unite us as the people of God in the body of Christ and as members of the family of Saint Vincent? How can we avoid tribal rivalry and strife?

4. What form will community living take in Africa? What will be the structures of dialogue? How will our lifestyles and our houses give witness to the simplicity to which the gospels call us? What are the ways of living together as "brothers who love one another deeply" (CR VIII, 2)? What will our local community plans be like?

5. What are the most appropriate prayer-forms for Africa? The Church in Africa is already developing a liturgy that is well inculturated, with their own styles of prayer, of song, of dance, of symbols, of gestures. Are there ways too in which our community prayer spaces, as well as our prayer forms, can truly reflect the African culture? Mental prayer, for example, was very important to Saint Vincent. He proposed a method for meditating that flowed from the culture in which he lived. What are the methods that are most useful within the African culture, for listening to God, reflecting on his gifts to us, and speaking with him?

Formation is crucial. Our evangelizing mission in Africa depends on it. Our community life will be vital only if we are well formed as members of an African apostolic family. Our prayer will be genuine only if it takes forms that touch the African heart.

I place these challenges before you with great confidence. Our Congregation has a long, rich history in Africa. Many wonderful Missionaries have come here and many of them are still here. Many generous young African candidates have entered our Company. This gives me reason for great confidence. I offer you these challenges today, because I trust that you will receive them with open hearts, with creativity, and with responsibility. The Church and the Congregation have a great future here in Africa. It lies in your hands and in your hearts.

To the
Company of the
Daughters of Charity

My Hopes for the Company of the Daughters of Charity[1]

Over the past year many Daughters of Charity have asked me to express my hopes for the Company, as I did a year ago for the Congregation of the Mission. I have hesitated for a very obvious reason: I am not a Daughter of Charity. I have never lived your life, even if at times I have shared in your joys and your sorrows. But I speak today because you, through your Constitutions, have asked me to be the Superior General of your Company. I also speak because I love the Company of the Daughters of Charity deeply. Some of the best women I have ever known live in your midst. With the freedom of one who loves, therefore, I will throw caution to the wind and will speak to you from the heart, trusting in your understanding.

What I express to you today is not a list of "impossible dreams." It is a list of hopes. I think that all of them are realizable, though surely with some difficulty.

1. *I hope that the international character of the Daughters of Charity will be deepened.*

The Company was already international in the time of Saint Vincent. He sent Sisters to Poland. As you know he sent Missionaries to Algeria, Madagascar, Poland, Italy, Ireland, Scotland, and also dreamed of the Indies, of Canada, of China. But, in reality, the Church has become a "world Church" only in the twentieth century. Vatican II, as Karl Rahner points out, is really the first "world Council."[2] Likewise, it is only in the twentieth century that the Daughters of Charity have become a worldwide Company with provinces on all the continents and on the pacific islands.

In this regard, a remarkable shift has taken place in the latter part of

---

1. Talk to the Visitatrixes and Regional Superiors of the Daughters of Charity in Paris, September 21, 1994.
2. K. Rahner, "The Abiding Significance of the Second Vatican Council," in *Theological Investigations* XX, 90-102; cf. also "The Future of the Church and the Church of the Future" in *Theological Investigations* XX, 103-14.

the twentieth century. Since 1970, for the first time in history, more than fifty percent of the world's Catholics are living in the southern hemisphere.[3] Walbert Bühlmann calls this the "coming of the third Church."[4]

In order to realize this hope, I want to encourage every Sister and every province to have a global awareness. Let me mention three signs that will witness to global awareness in the Company.

A first, concrete sign is the ability to respond to emergencies. Actually, many Daughters of Charity have been heroic in this regard in places like Somalia, Sudan, Sierra Leone, Cambodia, Guatemala, and Rwanda. Do not let provincial ties and provincial needs hold you back. When the needs of the Church are greater elsewhere, go with liberty.

A second sign of the international character of the Company, and of global awareness, is solidarity among the provinces. I urge you to cooperate with one another. This is already taking place through national and regional meetings of Visitatrixes, but I especially want to encourage you to cooperate in regard to the formation of candidates and in regard to assistance to poorer provinces. There are some things we can do together that we cannot do separately. Those of us who are better off materially can surely be of great assistance to those who have less.

Thirdly, a healthy sign of global awareness in the Company will be the presence of sisters from all the continents, with their varied races, here in the General Curia. An international Company needs ties between the center and the provinces. As the provinces of the "Third Church" grow, good communication with the center will be an utter necessity.

2. *That its missionary character be highlighted.*

The Mother General has already addressed this subject in her letter of January 6, 1994. This means that the Company will be mobile, flexible, responsive to the needs of the worldwide Church.

When the Company was founded, Saint Vincent and Saint Louise scattered tiny seeds—parish sodalities, so to speak—throughout France and then in Poland. Today the Company, by God's blessing, is a huge tree under whose branches the poor in eighty-four countries take shelter. Some of its most fruitful branches are in distant lands.

I pose this question: Could every province of the Daughters of Charity

---

3. W. Bühlmann, *The Church of the Future* (Maryknoll: Orbis, 1986) 4-5.
4. Cf. W. Bühlmann, *The Coming of the Third Church* (Slough, England: St. Pauls, 1976.

take on the responsibility for a mission outside its own territory? Could the Company become missionary not just territorially, but in the heart and will of its members, showing great flexibility in moving to wherever the needs of the poor cry out, both within one's province and outside?

One of the signs that the Company is filled with a missionary spirit will be the willingness to relinquish works that are well-established but which others can carry on, in order to free sisters for more pressing needs that others are unwilling or unable to meet.

3. *That there be a more concrete collaboration with lay people, especially the young.*

Pope John Paul II has often spoken of the generosity and the yearnings of young people. Echoing the words of Vatican II,[5] he calls young people "the hope of the Church."[6] He encourages us to reach out to them, to offer them a challenge. My predecessor, Fr. McCullen, repeated this theme several times in his addresses. I want to reaffirm it today.

It is not easy to work with young people. They ask challenging questions. Their ways seem different. Sometimes they appear to lack the discipline and the permanence of commitment that older people expect from others.

But young people hold the key to the future. They will be the Church of tomorrow. They are the twenty-first century's evangelizers of the poor. The inevitable, universal fact of human existence is that each of us passes on. We must, therefore, hand on the future to the young.

I challenge every province, even every work if possible, to reach out to young people. Involve them especially in the service of the poor. Involve them in your prayer and your reflection on the gospels. Involve them in some form of community living. All these things—service, prayer, community—are among the deepest aspirations of young people.

Today my hope is that you reach out to the young, wherever you labor. Share with them your wonderful charism. The strength and the charm of youth, Pope Paul VI said at the end of Vatican II, is "the ability to rejoice with what is beginning, to give oneself unreservedly, to renew oneself, and to set out again for new conquests."[7]

---

5. *Gravissimum Educationis*, 2.
6. *Origins,* vol. 14, n. 43 (April 11, 1985) 712.
7. Closing Message of Vatican II, *AAS* 58 (1966) 18.

In placing this pastoral objective before you, I do not make vocational recruitment its motivation but, at the same time, I suspect that if we work generously with the young they will be drawn to be servants of the poor. But let me also add an explicit word about vocations. Let your joy, your care for one another, your faith-filled lives, your service of the poor proclaim to young women the richness of your vocation. Encourage them. It is not easy for young people today to make permanent commitments. Say to them how deep God's love is and how good it is to share it with the poor.

4. That each province develop concrete models for community living.

You are a community *for the mission.* I am convinced that the quality of community living affects the quality of pastoral service to others. The gospels tell us that there is no greater sign of the presence of Christ in the world than a vibrant love for one another. The rule of Saint Vincent[8] and your present Constitutions speak of the affection you should have for one another.[9]

My concern is this. In recent years, it seems to me, we have been able to find a considerable number of renewed, creative ways of serving the poor. But, along with many other Communities, we have had much difficulty in finding ways of significantly renewing community living.

Many of the practices and structures that gave shape to community living in an earlier era have disappeared. In almost all cases, we could surely not now return to those same structures. Most of them served their purpose in their own time, but gradually became over-formalized, inflexible, and out-dated. Still, they often aimed at values that have abiding validity: unity with one another, common vision and energy in the apostolate, prayer, *revision de vie,* penance and conversion. With the passing away of former practices, however, we have unfortunately not yet come up with sufficient contemporary means for forming "New Communities."

Having visited, at one time or another, all of the continents, I see that it is quite difficult to envision a single model of community living.

One of the principal means that your Constitutions envision toward the building up of a living community is the local community plan.[10] This plan is, in a sense, a covenant entered into by the members of the local community,

---

8. *Rules of the Daughters of Charity* V, 1.
9. *Constitutions of the Daughters of Charity* 2.17.
10. *Ibid.,* 3.46.

by which they pledge to work toward certain common goals and engage in certain common practices. It is to include all aspects of community living and to be evaluated and revised periodically.[11] The Constitutions leave considerable flexibility to the local community for fleshing this plan out.

I encourage each of the provinces, and each of the Visitatrixes, to work creatively at evolving models for local community plans. These models should be flexible and demanding at the same time. I say *flexible*, because they will vary from culture to culture and place to place. But I say *demanding* because we commit ourselves to living together. In speaking with married couples, we often encourage them to be with their children, to eat with them, to instruct them, to recreate with them, to listen to them. We may even warn them that, if they neglect to do so, their bonds with the children will eventually be strained and broken. Analogously, if we neglect our Sisters in community, if we fail to be present to them, if we fail to share with them the key elements that constitute our life together (our apostolic mission, our prayer, our attentiveness to mutual listening and service), the bonds of our union will gradually be dissolved.

Working up good models of community living is a demanding objective. It will require creativity and discipline (two qualities that are not easily married!).

5. *That the Company will continue to emphasize and find creative means for integral formation on both initial and ongoing levels.*

Such integral formation would have various aspects: human, spiritual, apostolic, Vincentian, biblical, theological, professional. On all levels, the person herself will be seen as the one primarily responsible for her own formation.

I encourage you to be especially attentive to the formation of Sisters in the early years after the seminary. Bring them together often. Help them build a deep spiritual foundation, a rootedness in God. It is only in this way that they will be fully alive and persevering in the service of the poor.

6. *I would hope that the Company could develop prayer forms which are "something beautiful for God" and attractive to the young.*

I would like to see the following principles guide the preparation and the practice of your daily prayer:

---

11. *Statutes of the Daughters of Charity* 57.

 a. it should be beautiful
 b. it should be simple
 c. it should be attuned to the prayer of the Church
 d. it should be flavored by the tradition of the Company
 e. it should be flexible (adaptable to various situations).

Could each province and each house work at creating a daily common prayer that has these characteristics?

 7. *I hope that the sick poor will always have a privileged place in the mission of the Company and in each of its provinces.*

The sick poor are often the poorest of the poor, and today with maladies like AIDS, the most abandoned. I ask you to remember this: The mission of the Daughter of Charity is intimately bound up with the sick poor. Of course, over the centuries the charity of Christ drove the Daughters to serve many others in distress, but the foundational inspiration of the first Daughters of Charity was to give their whole lives in the service of the sick poor. Marguerite Naseau was the model Saint Vincent held up before the Company. She lived and died for the sick poor, because in 1633, at the age of 39, after having placed in her own bed a patient afflicted with plague, she succumbed to the plague herself. Saint Vincent loved to tell the story of this first Daughter of Charity. She inspired hundreds of thousands of others who would follow in her footsteps.

The original approbation of the Company, dated November 20, 1646, and signed by the Archbishop of Paris, reinforces this focus on the sick poor: "God has inspired [these young women] to dedicate themselves to the service of the sick poor."[12] The original statutes of the Company say the very same thing: This small group, which Saint Vincent de Paul originally envisioned as a parish sodality and which later was to become an enormous community, are called "servants of the sick poor."[13]

 8. *I hope that every Daughter of Charity will give primacy to these words of Saint Vincent: "The Daughter of Charity is a Daughter of God."*

Your name is Daughter of Charity. It means Daughter of God, Saint Vincent said, because God is charity.[14] Never forget that name. Seek to

12. *La Compagnie des Filles de la Charité aux origines*, présentation par Soeur Elisabeth Charpy (Paris, 1989) 440.
13. *Ibid.*, 441.
14. Cf. SV IX 14, 27, 59, 143, 149, 153, 210, 227, 435; X 128, 490, 501.

be well-informed, skilled nurses, teachers, administrators. But be known also as someone who brings God's peace into the room of the sick person, and deep faith and understanding into the meetings of the parish. Remember that it is only because of your love that the poor will recognize you for who you are. Let the poor sense in you the presence of God, as they did in Saint Louise. In the end, let them be able to say of you: "She walked with God. She was a true Daughter of Charity."

Those are my hopes, my sisters. I ask you to join with me in making them a reality.

Simplicity in the Life
of the Daughter of Charity[1]

For Vincent de Paul, simplicity, humility, and charity constitute the spirit of the Daughters of Charity (SV IX, 594-95). The word *spirit*, of course, means *life*. These three virtues are so important that without them a Daughter of Charity is "dead." Even if she is a dogged worker on behalf of the poor, even if she is a tireless organizer of service programs—if she lacks these three virtues, Saint Vincent would say, she is not a Daughter of Charity.

I will divide this chapter into three parts: 1) a brief study of simplicity as understood by Saint Vincent; 2) a description of a horizon-shift that has taken place in theology and spirituality between the seventeenth and twentieth centuries and that affects our way of viewing simplicity today; 3) an attempt at retrieving simplicity in contemporary forms.

Simplicity as Understood by Saint Vincent[2]

For Saint Vincent, simplicity is first of all, speaking the truth (CR II, 4; XII, 172). It is saying things as they are (SV I, 144), without concealing or hiding anything (SV I, 284; V, 464). He expresses this in a letter to François du Coudray on November 6, 1634:

> You know that your own kind heart has given me, thanks be to God, full liberty to speak to you with the utmost confidence, without any concealment or disguise; and it seems to me that up to the present you have recognized that fact in all my

1. Talk to the Daughters of Charity at the Motherhouse in Paris, August 15, 1993.
2. For some interesting information on this same subject, as well as further bibliography, the reader may wish to consult: J.-P. Renouard, "L'Esprit de la Congrégation: Les Vertus Fondamentales," *Vincentiana* XXVIII (1984) 599-615; cf. also T. Davitt, "The Five Characteristic Virtues," *Colloque XIV* (Autumn 1986) 109-120; A. Orcajo, *El Seguimiento de Jesús según Vicente de Paúl* (Caracas, 1988) 174-228. Cf. also Christian Sens, "Comme Prêtre Missionaire," in *Monsieur Vincent, Témoin de L'Evangile* (Toulouse, 1990) 133-151, esp. 140f.

dealings with you. My God! Am I to fall into the misfortune of being forced to do or to say in my dealings with you anything contrary to holy simplicity? Oh! Sir! May God preserve me from doing so in regard to anything whatsoever! It is the virtue I love most, the one to which in all my actions I pay most heed, so it seems to me; and if it were lawful to say so, the one, I may say, in which I have, by God's mercy, made some progress. (SV I, 284)

The heart must not think one thing while the mouth says another (SV IX, 81; IX, 605; XII, 172). Missionaries and Daughters of Charity must avoid all duplicity, dissimulation, cunning, and double meaning (SV II, 340; IX, 81).

For myself, I don't know, but God gives me such a great esteem for simplicity that I call it my gospel. I have a particular devotion and consolation in saying things as they are. (SV IX, 606)

Simplicity also consists in referring things to God alone (CR II, 4), or purity of intention (SV XII, 172). In this sense simplicity is doing everything for love of God and for no other end (SV XII, 174; XII, 302; II, 315). It entails avoiding "human respect" (SV II, 340), or doing things merely to look good in the eyes of others.

Simplicity involves an unadorned lifestyle. We fail against simplicity, Saint Vincent tells us, when our rooms are filled with superfluous furniture, pictures, large numbers of books, and vain and useless things (SV XII, 175). We must use with great simplicity the things that have been given to us (SV IX, 607).

Simplicity also entails explaining the gospel by familiar comparisons (SV XI, 50). When he speaks to the Daughters of Charity, he uses the Little Method that was employed in the Congregation of the Mission at that time (CR XII, 5). Preaching about a virtue, for example, he might present:

— motives for living it,
— its nature or definition, and
— means for putting it into practice. (SV XI, 260)

e. In Saint Vincent's mind, simplicity is very closely linked with humility (SV I, 144) and it is inseparable from prudence (CR II, 5), which for him means always basing one's judgment on the evangelical maxims or on the judgments of Jesus Christ (SV XII, 169, 176). Both prudence and simplicity tend toward the same goal: to speak and to act well (SV XII, 176).

A Significant Horizon Shift [3]

Perspective makes a huge difference. Much depends on where we stand. My view of Paris is altogether different from the top of the Eiffel Tower than it is from the bottom of a metro station. It is the same with theology and spirituality. Our horizons change from one era to another, and they affect our way of seeing God and seeing the world.

Horizon shifts, whether we react to them favorably or unfavorably, necessarily have an impact on the way we see all reality. They bring with them gains and losses, as we interpret life, people, truth and events from a changed historical perspective. Practices that seemed apt in one era may seem quaint in another, because our way of viewing them has changed quite dramatically. So it is with the three virtues that constitute the spirit of the Daughters of Charity. Putting this in traditional language, we might say that the challenge is to find the substance of each of the virtues, to put aside those concrete ("accidental") forms that are no longer appropriate for mediating that substance in the modern world, and to find contemporary forms which will embody it more readily.

Of course, not all practices of a previous era are irrelevant today; in fact, many that Saint Vincent suggested are still suitable means for expressing the values he sought. Yet just as many languages cease to exist as a living word capable of communicating meaning, so also some of the practices that were once suitable vehicles for expressing values in Saint Vincent's time are no longer capable of doing so now. In those cases, the challenge is to find or create new forms that will do the job.

A significant shift which has taken place between Saint Vincent's time and ours is that change has come to find a greater place in our expectations. People today are willing to accept fewer absolutes. They question absolute prohibitions which were formerly accepted. They emphasize that changing circumstances make one case different from another.

---

3. For a treatment of the nature and importance of horizon-shifts, cf. my articles entitled "Five Characteristic Virtues: Yesterday and Today," *Vincentiana* XXIX (1985) 226-54; "The Four Vincentian Vows: Yesterday and Today," *Vincentiana* XXXIV (1990) 230-307.

Another has been increasing pluralism. Contemporary thinkers recognize the value of different cultures, philosophies, and theologies. The inductive scientific method emphasizes the *search for truth*, whereas formerly a more philosophical method emphasized the *possession of truth*. An obvious sign of this in ecclesial matters is the ecumenical movement.

This way of viewing truth also has implications in regard to the virtue of simplicity.

Simplicity Today

In some ways simplicity is not difficult to retrieve today. The virtue which Saint Vincent loved most, his "gospel," so to speak, still appeals. In a contemporary context described above, it can take many forms, some of which are suggested below.

a. *Speaking the truth.* Simplicity today, as in Saint Vincent's time, means saying things as they are.

Truth is a keystone concept. Truth is the foundation of trust, which is the basis of all human relations; falsehood, on the other hand, violates trust and makes genuine human relationships impossible.

But experience proves that it is very difficult to let our *yes* mean *yes* and our *no* mean *no*, as Jesus puts it (Mt 5:37; cf. Jas 5:12; 2 Cor 1:17-20). It is precisely because Jesus speaks the truth that his enemies give him no credence (Jn 8:44). Ultimately, he dies for the truth.

On the other hand, as Saint Vincent reminds us, there is a great attractiveness about those who speak the truth. We sense spontaneously that they have nothing to conceal, that they have no hidden agendas. They are truly free. Consequently, it is easy to relate to them.

Yet speaking the truth with consistency is an extremely difficult discipline. We are tempted to blur the truth when our own convenience is at stake or when the truth is embarrassing to us personally. It is also difficult to be true to one's word, one's promises, one's commitments. When we make a statement in the present, it is either true or false right then and there. When we make a commitment for the future, however, it is true only to the extent that we keep it true. Truth, in this sense, is fidelity. It is in this sense especially that Jesus is true to us. He promises to be, and is with us always, even to the end. It is in this same sense that we are called to be true to vows, to friendships, to our concrete commitments to serve.

Speaking the truth is especially important in the relationship we call "spiritual direction." We choose a "soul friend" so that, with his or her help, we might grow in the Lord's life and in discerning those things which promote his kingdom. It is imperative, therefore, that this relationship be characterized by free self-disclosure and by the avoidance of "hidden corners" in our lives. No one is an island. We need others to mirror back to us what is happening or not happening in our journey toward the Lord. The quality of such relationships in spiritual direction will depend largely upon the simplicity with which we disclose ourselves.

b. *Witnessing to the truth.* This understanding of simplicity is most relevant. People spontaneously admire those who live out what they believe and say. A very comprehensive survey in regard to priests and ministers has disclosed that the quality people most seek in ministers is genuineness, authenticity.[4]

In an era when so many young people have lost confidence in civil and religious authorities because of corruption and proved duplicity (e.g., the political scandals in Italy, Spain, France, England, the United States, and so many other countries), those whose lives match their words speak more powerfully than ever. Speaking and witnessing to the truth are central Christian values, especially in John's gospel. Jesus is the truth (Jn 4:6). The person who acts in the truth comes into the light (Jn 3:21). When the Spirit comes, he will guide us to all truth (Jn 16:13). It is the truth that sets us free (Jn 8:32). The reason why Jesus has come is to testify to the truth (Jn 18:37). Anyone who is of the truth hears his voice (Jn 18:37).

This type of simplicity is also extremely attractive in the modern world. Young people love those who are "real," "genuine." These are contemporary names for simplicity.

c. *Seeking the truth.* Being "real" or genuine today, as is evident from the horizon-shift described above, may often demand our admission that we are groping to find the truth, that we are uncertain as to the truth, or that there are complementary truths. This is all the more necessary in a world where it is not longer possible to have universal knowledge.

We are conscious today of being wayfarers. Life is a journey, an

---

4. Association of Theological Schools in the United States and Canada, *Readiness for Ministry* (Vandalia, 1975-76).

ongoing process. So it is also with the quest for truth. We grasp the truth gradually. It is not captured in a single insight. Our verbal attempts at expressing it are always limited, perfectible. Nor is it possessed once for all. It is constructed bit by bit. The deeper we descend into the well, the deeper we know the well to be. So we must be dedicated to seeking, pursuing, finding the truth. This virtue, which Bernard Häring calls "dedication to the truth," takes the form of listening well, meeting and discussing with others, reading, ongoing education.

d. *Being in the truth.* This is what we might traditionally call simplicity of intention, purity of heart, referring all things to God. It is single-minded devotion to the Lord and his kingdom. In this sense, when the simple person labors, he labors because he loves God and he loves his people. He does not labor in order to be placed in high positions. Nor does he labor because admiration or money may come his way if he takes on extra work. When a simple person recognizes that his motives are mixed, he talks them out and seeks the aid of another to help him discern why he is really doing things. He knows that it is impossible always to have a single intention, but he seeks to make love of God and service of the neighbor the dominant motive in everything. Jesus groped to know his Father's will and struggled with contrary desires as he resolved to do it; the simple person today will necessarily engage in and work through a similar struggle.

As an aid in growing in this type of simplicity it is helpful to survey the competing values in our lives from time to time. Comfort, power, popularity, and financial security can subtly compete with love of God and love of neighbor. Sometimes these secondary motives will coincide with purer motives (as when the people whom we serve admire us and give us lots of positive feedback). But when they conflict, are we willing to sacrifice?

e. *Practicing the truth (in love).* This means performing works of justice and charity, making the truth come alive creatively in the world. It means bringing the truth to completion in deed. It means making our word become flesh, giving the gospels concrete life-form. The truth cannot just be verbal; it must be lived. Commitments to do the works of justice cannot just be spoken; they must be kept, day in and day out. The gospels cannot just be preached; they must be practiced in love.

Simplicity, from this point of view, means that when we preach justice we must also live justice. When we preach solidarity with the poor, we must also live in solidarity with the poor. When we exhort others to a simple life-style, we must live simply ourselves. When we say that we are celibate, we must live as celibates. When we proclaim the ways of peace-making, we must act as peace-makers.

f. *Integration.* Simplicity in this sense means personal wholeness, the ability to bring together in a unified way the varied aspects of one's life: labor, prayer, community, solitude, leisure. Young people speak of "having it together." Formation literature today often stresses integration as the goal of the whole formation process.

Martin Buber tells a striking story that illustrates the importance of integration:

> A hasid of the Rabbi of Lublin once fasted from one Sabbath to the next. On Friday afternoon he began to suffer such cruel thirst that he thought he would die. He saw a well, went up to it, and prepared to drink. But instantly he realized that because of one brief hour he had still to endure, he was about to destroy the work of the entire week. He did not drink and went away from the well. Then he was touched by a feeling of pride for having passed this difficult test. When he became aware of it, he said to himself, "Better I go and drink than let my heart fall prey to pride." He went back to the well, but just as he was going to bend down to draw water, he noticed that his thirst had disappeared. When the Sabbath had begun, he entered his teacher's house. "Patchwork!" the rabbi called to him, as he crossed the threshold.[5]

The truly simple person arrives at "being a united soul." His life is no longer "patchwork," but is "all of a piece." Love of God and love of neighbor come together in a single whole.

g. *Simplicity of life.* As in Saint Vincent's time, simplicity today also has implications in regard to life-style. Some contemporary writers even prefer to use the terminology "simplicity of life" to "poverty" when speaking of the content of our vow. Regardless of the terminology, our commitment to community for the service of the poor necessarily in-

---

5. Martin Buber, "Resolution," in *The Way of Man According to the Teaching of the Hasidism* 21.

volves a commitment to a simple life-style, in which we share, at least in some ways, in the experience of those in need.

But such simplicity of life must not be confused, as sometimes happens, with drabness or lack of beauty (or worse, with lack of cleanliness!). On the contrary, simplicity implies beauty and enhances it. Simplicity is one of the characteristics of genuine art. Masterpieces of painting, sculpture, design, and music, even when quite complex, maintain a radical simplicity that lies at the heart of their beauty. Consequently, it is important to foster a sense of "the beautiful" in our lives. Especially the places and the forms of our prayer (singing, methods of reciting the psalms, images, etc.), while simple, should be "something beautiful for God."

Humility in the Life
of the Daughter of Charity[1]

Humility, along with simplicity and charity, is one of the virtues that constitute the spirit of the Daughters of Charity.

This chapter will be divided into three parts: 1) a brief study of humility as understood by Saint Vincent; 2) a description of a horizon-shift that has taken place in theology and spirituality between the seventeenth and twentieth centuries and that affects our way of viewing humility today; 3) an attempt at retrieving humility in contemporary forms.

Humility as Understood by Saint Vincent

For Saint Vincent, humility is the recognition that all good comes from God. He writes to Firmin Get on March 8, 1658: "Let us no longer say: it is I who have done this good work; for every good thing ought to be done in the name of our Lord Jesus Christ" (SV VII, 98-99). "Be very much on your guard against attributing anything to yourself. By doing so you would commit robbery and do injury to God, who alone is the author of every good thing," he writes to Jacques Pesnelle on October 15, 1658 (SV VII, 289). God pours out his abundant gifts on the humble "who recognize that all good which is done by them comes from God" (SV I, 182).

Our sins too should help us grow in humility (SV XI, 397). Humility is recognition of our own lowliness and faults (CR II, 7), accompanied by exuberant confidence in God (SV III, 279; V, 165; II, 233, 336; X, 201; IX, 382). In writing to Charles Nacquart on March 22, 1648, about the gift of vocation, he states: "Humility alone is capable of receiving this grace. A perfect abandonment of everything that you are and can be in the exuberant confidence in your sovereign creator ought to follow" (SV III, 279).

Humility involves voluntary self-emptying (SV V, 534; XI, 61, 312; XII,

---

1. Talk to the Daughters of Charity at the Motherhouse in Paris, January 1, 1994.

200). This entails loving to be unknown and abandoned (SV VII, 312; X, 129, 152; XII, 709). It means avoiding the applause of the world (SV I, 496; IX, 605; X, 148). It involves taking the last place (SV IX, 605) and loving the hidden life (SV IX, 680).

Humility involves esteeming others as more worthy than yourself (SV V, 37; IX, 303). In this regard, it is a communal virtue, not just an individual one. We are to regard the Company as the least of all (SV IX, 303; X, 200; XI, 60, 114-15, 434; XII, 438).

Saint Vincent gives numerous motives for the practice of humility:

* He notes that Jesus was humble and happy to be seen as the least of men. (SV I, 182, 534; XI, 400)

* It is the characteristic virtue of Jesus (SV XI, 400), and should be the characteristic virtue of a true Daughter of Charity. (SV X, 527)

* The saints too were humble; "It is the virtue of Jesus Christ, the virtue of his holy mother, the virtue of the greatest of the saints." (SV XI, 56-57)

* God blesses humble beginnings. (SV II, 281; V, 487)

* "Humility is the origin of all the good that we do." (SV IX, 674)

* God has called us, lowly people, to do great things. (SV X, 128, 198)

* It is the arms by which we conquer the devil (SV I, 536; XI, 312), since the devil and pride are the same. (SV IX, 706)

* We cannot persevere without humility. (SV I, 528; X, 528; XII, 304)

* It brings all other virtues with it. (SV XII, 210)

* It is the foundation of all evangelical perfection, the node of the whole spiritual life. (CR II, 7)

* Everyone loves it (SV XII, 197), but it is easier to think about than to practice. (SV XI, 54)

* It is the source of peace and union. (SV XII, 106, 210)

* If the Company possesses humility, it will be a paradise:

"If you establish yourselves in it, what will happen? You will make of this company a paradise and people will likely say that it is a group of the happiest people on earth." (SV X, 439)

* Heaven is won by humility. (CR II, 6)

Saint Vincent suggested many means for acquiring humility:

* We should do acts of humility daily. (SV IX, 680; XII, 716; I, 183)

* We should confess our faults openly (SV V, 164; XI, 54) and accept the admonitions of others. (CR X 13-14)

* We should desire to be admonished. (SV IX, 382)

* We should pray to our Lord and the Blessed Mother as models of humility. (SV IX, 680; XI, 56-57)

* We should believe that we are the worst in the world. (SV X, 552)

* We should recognize that everyone has his faults; then there will be little trouble excusing others. (SV X, 438)

* We should preach Jesus Christ and not ourselves. (SV XII, 22)

* Superiors should so act that others will not be able to tell that they are superiors. (SV XI, 346; IX, 302)

A Significant Horizon Shift: A More Positive Attitude Toward Creation and Less Emphasis on Sin

The struggle with Jansenism greatly influenced seventeenth-century thinking. Theologians and spiritual writers, while combatting Jansenism, were influenced by many of its presuppositions. It was "in the air they breathed," so to speak. Like Manicheanism and Albigensianism, two of its predecessors, it had a very negative view of created reality. It was overly rigorous and focused on sin. The twentieth century has brought a renewed emphasis on the dignity of the human person and on the goodness of creation. This is particularly evident in *Gaudium et Spes* (9,

12, 22) and the writings of John Paul II.[2] Theologians and spiritual writers take a much more positive attitude toward "the human." The human person is seen as the center of creation. Created realities are extensions of his being and ways in which he celebrates and shares God's gifts. The shadow side of this horizon-shift is that it has brought with it a deepening loss of the sense of sin. Consequently, among young people especially, there is a diminished consciousness of the need for mortification and penance. The twentieth century has witnessed increased sexual permissiveness in society and a weakening of family structures. In some parts of the world, one out of two marriages ends in divorce. The number of single-parent families is huge. In some cities more than half the children are born out of wedlock. Abortion is widespread.

Both the bright and the shadow side of this horizon-shift have implications for the virtue of humility.

Humility Today

Because of the horizon-shift just mentioned, it is difficult for modern men and women to accept Saint Vincent's language when he speaks about humility. We tend to cringe when he calls himself the worst of all sinners and speaks of his community as the most wretched in the world.

Yet when he emphasizes humility, prescinding from the language in which he speaks, Saint Vincent penetrates a basic, abiding New Testament truth. Luke's gospel, in particular, tells us that God comes to the lowly, the poor of Israel, those who recognize their need for him and long for him. In this sense, humility is "the foundation of all evangelical perfection, the node of the whole spiritual life" (CR II, 7). In this sense too, Saint Vincent went to the core of the gospels when he said that "humility is the origin of all the good that we do" (SV IX, 674).

Moving beyond Saint Vincent's language and a rhetoric that was characteristic of the seventeenth century, it is important to articulate an understanding of humility and the contemporary forms that it takes.

a. Humility is a recognition of our creatureliness and our redeemedness, both being gifts of God's love.

---

2. Cf. *Redemptor Hominis, passim.*

We are completely dependent upon the Lord. "In him we live and move and have our being" (Acts 17:28). There is nothing that we have not received. "Truly you have formed my inmost being; you knit me in my mother's womb" (Ps 139:13). Whatever we are, whatever we do, whatever we possess comes from the Lord. We are also very much dependent on others. The modern age is increasingly conscious of the interdependence of all men and women. The humble person recognizes interdependence both as a sign of his limitedness and as a source of enrichment. We need others and cannot do without them. In solidarity with them, we journey toward the kingdom.

Besides being created beings, we are sinners who have been redeemed through God's gracious love. "All have sinned and are deprived of the glory of God. All are now undeservedly justified by the gift of God, through the redemption wrought in Christ Jesus" (Rom 3:23-24).

Perhaps as a distorted reaction to an overemphasis on sin in the past, the modern age has difficulty sustaining a sense of sin. Yet sin, if we are alert to it, shows itself in numerous different ways in our lives: in our prejudices, in our tendency to categorize other people indiscriminately, in our speaking lightly about others' negative points, in our slowness to pray, in our inability to get excited about gospel values, in our selectivity in reading the gospels, in our unwillingness to share what we have with the poor, in our hesitancy to divest ourselves of power and to stand with the needy in their misery, in our compliance with unjust social structures. In face of all this, the Lord forgives us eagerly and gives us life in Christ Jesus. It is not by the works we do that we are saved, but rather by the gift of God in Christ Jesus (cf. Gal 2:21-22). Otherwise grace is not grace (Rom 11:6).

b. Humility is gratitude for gifts. In the New Testament, gratitude is the opposite side of the coin from humility. The person who has received all stands before the Lord in a spirit of thanksgiving. In this sense, thanksgiving is the central Christian attitude, which we daily celebrate as eucharist.

Mary epitomizes this attitude in Luke's gospel:

My being proclaims the greatness of the Lord.
My spirit finds joy in God my Savior
for he has looked upon his servant in her lowliness.

All ages to come shall call me blessed.
God who is mighty has done great things for me.
Holy is his name.
His mercy is from age to age on those who fear him.

(Luke 1:46-50)

Mary cries out in praise and thanksgiving for the many gifts that God has given her. She recognizes God's gifts, without diminishing or denying them, and responds with gratitude. In this she echoes the psalmist: "Give thanks to the Lord for he is good, for his loving kindness endures forever. Give thanks to the God of gods for his loving kindness endures forever" (Ps 136:1-3).

This type of gratitude characterizes the poor. Henri Nouwen writes:

> Many poor people live in such close relationship with the many rhythms of nature that all the goods that come to them are experienced as free gifts of God. Children and friends, bread and wine, music and pictures, trees and flowers, water and life, a house, a room with just one bed, all are gifts to be grateful for and celebrated. This basic sense I have come to know. I am always surrounded by words of thanks, "Thanks for your visit, your blessing, your sermon, your prayer, your gifts, your presence with us." Even the smallest and most necessary goods are a reason for gratitude. This all-pervading gratitude is the basis for celebration. The poor not only are grateful for life, they also celebrate life constantly.[3]

Today those responsible for formation know the importance of an awareness of one's gifts as part of a positive self-image. But, almost in spite of the horizon-shift described above, the problem of negative self-image, which has nothing to do with genuine humility, remains a persistent one.

Recognizing that all is gift, the humble person will be eager to avoid comparisons. He or she will receive life with gratitude, leaving judgment to the Lord, as the gospels frequently exhort us to do (cf. Mt 7:1-5). Pride

---

3. Henri Nouwen, "Humility," in *America* (December 11, 1982) 372; cf. H. Nouwen, *Gracias* (San Francisco, 1983) 146-47.

loves comparison. The avaricious person may be satisfied when he possesses much; the proud person remains restless as long as anyone else has more. Humility spurns comparison. It can focus on the good in others, just as in oneself, and thank the Lord for it.

c. Humility involves a servant's attitude. This is central in the New Testament, especially for those who exercise authority. "If anyone wishes to be first, he must be the last of all and the servant of all" (Mk 9:35). In John's gospel Jesus demonstrates this for his disciples through a parable in action when he washes their feet.

> Do you understand what I just did for you? You address me as "teacher" and "Lord," and fittingly enough for that is what I am. But if I washed your feet—I your teacher and Lord— then you must wash each other's feet. What I just did was to give you an example: as I have done so you must do. (Jn 13:12-15)

We are called, like Jesus, "not to be served but to serve" (Mt 20:28). The expectation of the Church in the modern world is that authority figures will be collegial, dialogic, humble servants. An ancient Christian baptismal hymn captures this insight into Jesus and applies it to his followers:

> Your attitude must be that of Christ. Though he was in the form of God he did not deem equality with God something to be grasped at. Rather he emptied himself and took the form of a slave, being born in the likeness of men. He was known to be of human estate, and it was thus that he humbled himself, obediently accepting even death, death on a cross. Because of this God highly exalted him and bestowed on him the name above every other name, so that at Jesus' name every knee must bend in the heavens, on the earth, and under the earth, and every tongue proclaim to the glory of God the Father: Jesus Christ is Lord! (Phil 2:5-11)

As servants, we must be willing to do humble things. Today, leadership tasks that were once prestigious, like administration, may truly be humble tasks, exposing the servant-leader to much criticism while engaging her in many meetings and humdrum paper work that bring little positive feedback.

d. Humility also entails allowing ourselves to be evangelized by the poor ("our lords and masters" as Saint Vincent liked to call them). This insight, already present in the early Church and echoed later by Saint Vincent, receives great emphasis in Latin American theology and in an ecclesiology "from below."

Not only do we as ministers teach others, we must allow them to teach us. As Augustine put it, there are seeds of the Word everywhere and in everyone.[4] Only the humble can discern them. We must hear God speaking to us as we see the willingness of the poor to share the little that they have, as we see their gratitude to God for the simple gifts that he gives them, as we see their hoping against hope that God will provide, as we see their reverence and care and respect for us as well as for God. The poor will preach to us eloquently if we allow them.

As you can see, my sisters, humility is utterly fundamental for Saint Vincent. It is the foundation of all evangelical perfection; it is the node of the whole spiritual life (CR II, 7). He says with great clarity: "Humility—let it be your password!" (SV XII, 206)

---

4. Cf. *Evangelii Nuntiandi*, 53.

Charity in the Life
of the Daughter of Charity[1]

Saint Vincent describes the spirit of the Company very clearly (SV IX, 594-95):

> The spirit of your Company consists of three things: to love our Lord and to serve him in a spirit of humility and simplicity. As long as charity, humility and simplicity exist among you, it may be said that the Company is still alive.

Your Constitutions say the very same thing when they speak about the spirit of the Daughters of Charity: "The Evangelical virtues of humility, simplicity and charity are the path along which the Daughters of Charity should allow themselves to be guided by the Holy Spirit."[2]

I have already reflected with you on simplicity and humility. Today, let us focus on charity.

Charity: Developing a "Filial Relationship with the Father and Love for Our Neighbor"

Jesus' psychology, Saint Vincent writes in one of his letters, is caught up in two all-consuming directions, "his filial relationship with the Father and his charity toward the neighbor" (SV VI, 393).[3]

1. A filial relationship with the Father and docility to his providence.

"Let us give ourselves to God," Saint Vincent says repeatedly to the Daughters of Charity, as well as to the Vincentians (cf. SV IX, 26, 534, 592; X, 513; XII, 323, 354). He has deep confidence in God as his Father, into whose hands he can place himself and his works. The journal written

---

1. Talk to the Daughters of Charity at the Motherhouse in Paris, January 1, 1995.
2. *Constitutions of the Daughters of Charity*, 1.10
3. The French reads: ". . . religion vers son Père."

160

by Jean Gicquel recounts how Vincent told Frs. Alméras, Berthe and Gicquel, on June 7, 1660, just four months before his death: "To be consumed for God, to have no goods nor power except for the purpose of consuming them for God. That is what our Savior did himself, who was consumed for love of his Father" (SV XIII, 179).

Saint Vincent wanted love for God to be all-embracing. He writes to Pierre Escart: "I greatly hope we may set about stripping ourselves entirely of affection for anything that is not God, be attached to things only for God and according to God, and that we may seek and establish his kingdom first of all in ourselves, and then in others. That is what I entreat you to ask of him for me" (SV II, 106).

Because God loves us deeply as a Father, he exercises a continual providence in our lives. In a letter to Bernard Codoing, Saint Vincent states: "The rest will come in its time. Grace has its moments. Let us abandon ourselves to the providence of God and be very careful not to run ahead of it. If it pleases God to give me some consolation in our vocation it is this: that I think, so it seems to me, that we have tried to follow his great providence in everything" (SV II, 153). Likewise he writes to Saint Louise de Marillac: "My God, my daughter, what great hidden treasures there are in holy providence and how marvelously our Lord is honored by those who follow it and do not kick against it!" (SV I, 68; cf. III, 197).

Saint Vincent's teaching on providence rests on two foundation-stones: 1) deep confidence in God as a loving Father; 2) "indifference," that is, "willing only what he wills" (SV V, 402).

One senses in this focus on providence a distinctively Lucan emphasis.[4] The Spirit of God is active from the beginning in Luke, guiding the course of history. He anoints Jesus with power from on high and directs him and his disciples in their ministry."[5]

* The Holy Spirit will come down on you and the power of the Most High will overshadow you. (Lk 1:35)

* Having received baptism . . . the Holy Spirit descended on him. (Lk 3:22)

---

4. Cf. J. Shultz, "Gottes Vorsehung bei Lukas," *Zeitschrift für die neutestamentiche Wissenschaft* 54 (1963), 104-16.

5. The Book of Acts continues this theme of the "Gospel of the Holy Spirit". There are fifty-seven references to the Spirit in Acts; cf. Fitzmyer, *The Gospel According to Luke* 227.

* Jesus, filled with the Holy Spirit . . . was led by the Spirit into the desert. (Lk 4:1)

* Jesus returned to Galilee with the power of the Holy Spirit. (Lk 4:14)

* The Spirit of the Lord is upon me. (Lk 4:18)

* Jesus rejoiced in the Holy Spirit. (Lk 10:21)

* Your heavenly Father will give the Holy Spirit to those who ask him. (Lk 11:13)

* Whoever blasphemes against the Holy Spirit will not be forgiven. (Lk 12:10)

* The Holy Spirit will teach you at that moment what you should say. (Lk 12:12)

Trust in providence is confidence in a loving Father. It shows itself in the ability to see beyond particular events to a larger picture, in patient waiting, in perseverance. But providence is also honored, as Saint Vincent pointed out, by using the means that God places at our disposal for accomplishing his goals.[6] If someone should be tempted to interpret Saint Vincent's teaching on providence too passively, she might recall the founder's words to Edme Jolly (SV VII, 310): "You are one of the few who honor the providence of God very much by the preparation of remedies against foreseen evils. I thank you very humbly for this and pray that our Lord will continue to enlighten you more and more so that such enlightenment may spread through the Company."

Love for Christ in the person of the poor.[7]

While the Christ of Saint Vincent is "Lord" and "Son of God," he lives in the person of the poor. He continues to suffer in them (SV X, 680).

He says to the Daughters of Charity on February 13, 1646: "In serving the poor, you serve Jesus Christ. O my Daughters, how true that is! You serve Christ in the person of the poor. That is as true as the fact that we are here" (SV IX, 252; cf. X, 123). He frequently cites Matthew 25:31-46

---

6. SV V, 396: "Let us wait patiently, but let us act, and, as it were, let us make haste slowly."
7. On this same theme, cf. José-Maria Ibañez, "Le Pauvre, Icône de Jésus-Christ," in *Monsieur Vincent, Témoin de L'Evangile* (Toulouse, 1990) 155-68.

to reinforce the identification of Jesus with the poor:[8] "So this is what obliges you to serve them with respect, as your masters, and with devotion: that they represent for you the person of our Lord, who said: 'Whatever you do for one of these, the least of my brethren, I will consider it as done to me' " (SV X, 332).[9]

Because of this identification with Christ, the poor are "our lords and masters" (cf. SV IX, 119; X, 332). In drafting the rule for the Daughters, he writes that they should "love one another deeply, as sisters whom he has joined together with the bond of his love, and they should cherish the poor as their masters, since our Lord is in them, and they in Our Lord" (SV XIII, 540). He repeats the same theme to the priests and the brothers of the Mission: "Let us go then, my brothers, and work with a new love in the service of the poor looking even for the poorest and the most abandoned, recognizing before God that they are our lords and masters and that we are unworthy to render them our small services" (SV XI, 393). The Christ of Vincent, his "lord and master," is therefore to be found in the sick, the prisoner, the galley slave, the abandoned child, those ravaged by the religious wars of the day (SV X, 680).

Let me briefly mention two characteristics of love of neighbor, as taught by Saint Vincent to the Daughters of Charity.

a. The love of those living in the Vincentian spirit is to be both "affective and effective" (SV IX, 475, 592, 599; XI, 40). Saint Vincent repeats this theme over and over again. "The love of a Daughter of Charity is not only tender, it is effective, because they serve the poor effectively" (SV IX, 593).

b. They will minister to the poor "spiritually and corporally" (SV IX, 59, 593; XI, 364). This is clear not only in regard to the Daughters of Charity, but it is evident in the mandates that Saint Vincent gives to the various other groups he founded: the Congregation of the Mission, the Confraternities of Charity, and the Ladies of Charity. For Vincent, Jesus comes "to proclaim liberty to captives, recovery of sight to the blind and release to prisoners, to announce a year of favor from the Lord" (Lk 4:18). He comes to "save his people from their sins" (Mt 1:21; cf. Lk 1:77). The Daughter of Charity, therefore, will tend not only to bodily needs; she will share her faith by her witness and her words. Saint Vincent, more-

---

8. Cf. SV IX, 252, 324, 454; X, 332; XIII, 788, 790, 806; XII, 88, 100.
9. Cf. also SV X, 679-80.

over, warns the members of the Congregation of the Mission that they should not think of their mission in exclusively spiritual terms.[10] Rather, they too should care for the sick, the foundlings, the insane, even the most abandoned (SV XI, 393).

Today, the unity between evangelization and human promotion, so much a part of Saint Vincent's spirit, is one of the linchpins in the Church's social teaching.[11]

Some Means toward Practical Charity

The emphasis in the Vincentian tradition is on *practical* charity. Saint Vincent puts the accent on *effective* love. It is as if he hears Jesus saying: "When I was hungry, not only did you sympathize with me, you gave me to eat. When I was thirsty, not only did you look on me with compassion, but you gave me something to drink." From the origins of the Company right up to the present, the world has recognized in the Daughter of Charity a woman of practical, concrete, effective love. It is in this way that she shows herself a daughter of God, who is love. Let me suggest four ways of loving concretely.

1. Accepting the Lord's love

God's love comes first. We give only what we have received.

A number of superiors and those responsible for formation programs today attest that a negative self-image is the root of many of the problems with which members of communities struggle. This being the case, let me suggest that, along with healthy, loving human relationships, acceptance of the Lord's love is a key factor in the self-acceptance that enables us to love maturely. For many, work or achievements unfortunately play a disproportionate role in their feeling valued personally. But in the long

---

10. SV XII, 87: "If there are any among us who think they are in the Congregation of the Mission to preach the gospel to the poor but not to comfort them, to tend to their spiritual needs and not to their temporal needs, I respond that we ought to assist them and have them assisted in every way, by ourselves and by others . . . To do this is to preach the gospel by words and by works. . . ."

11. Cf. Synod of Bishops, 1971, *Justice in the World,* in *AAS* LXIII (1971) 924: "Action on behalf of justice and participation in the transformation of the world are integral elements in the preaching of the gospel." Cf. also, *Centesimus Annus, 5.*

run, genuine self-worth rests on a consciousness of the deep personal love of the Lord as Creator and Redeemer.

Meditation on some striking scriptural texts concerning the Lord's personal love for us is a very helpful means of growing in awareness of that love. In his struggles to be faithful, Moses, pleading for light and strength, heard these words from the Lord: "This request, too, which you have just made, I will carry out, because you have found favor with me and you are my intimate friend" (Ex 33:7-17).[12]

2. Labor

Servants get their hands dirty. They labor long and hard. They engage in difficult tasks as nurses, teachers, social workers, administrators. They are on the front lines in ministering to the poor.

In your ministry, as Saint Vincent says, first do and then teach. As a follower of Christ, a servant of the poor, you will touch the hearts of God's people especially when you give vibrant witness:

— through the language of works (cf. SV II, 4): performing the works of justice and mercy which are a sign that the kingdom of God is really alive among us: feeding the hungry, giving drink to the thirsty, helping to find the causes of their hunger and thirst and the ways of alleviating them;

— through the language of words: announcing with deep conviction the Lord's presence, his love, his offer of forgiveness and acceptance to all;

— through the language of relationships: being *with* the poor, working *with* them, forming a community that shows the Lord's love for all.

3. Creativity

Saint Vincent tells us that "Love is inventive to the point of infinity" (SV XI, 146). I have always admired the Daughters of Charity for your inventiveness. Because you live in daily contact with the poor you will

---

12. Among many other texts on which it might be helpful to meditate throughout our lives, I would suggest: Dt 1:29-33; 7:7-11; 8:5-10; 11:10-17; 32:10-11; Is 43:1-7; 49:14-16; 54:5-10; 55; Hos 11:1-9; Ps 103; 139; 145; Lk 7:36-50; 12:22-32; 15:11-32; Jn 3:16-17; 14:14-28; Eph 1:3-14; Jas 1:17-18; 1 Jn 4:9-10.

be among the first to know their real needs. It will not be I, who am sitting behind a desk or visiting the provinces. It will not be sociologists or economists, who study the needs of the poor by examining the data they receive. You will know ahead of us, because the poor tell you directly. I encourage you to continue to be inventive in the service of the needs that you discover. Ask the question individually and as a Community: What is this poor person asking of me concretely? What is the AIDS patient asking of the Daughter of Charity? What is the handicapped child asking? What is the refugee in a camp asking? What is the sick person in his or her home crying out for? Then be creative in ministering to his or her needs.

4. Perseverance

Love in practice, as Dorothy Day tells us, can be a harsh and dreadful thing compared with love in dreams.

It is easy to love for a time. It is difficult to love for life. Permanent commitment is more fragile today than it was in the seventeenth century, especially since many of the societal supports that undergirded it at that time have disappeared. So practical charity shows itself today especially as fidelity. It is gold tested in fire. It finds ways of loving both "in season and out of season." Practical charity adjusts, finding new ways and developing professionally, especially through ongoing formation. In this era of second careers and early retirement, it seeks to learn ways of expressing love for the Lord and love for the poor even in ministries that may be quite different from the ways in which one served in his or her youth. The challenge which persevering and adjusting present today was not unknown to Saint Vincent: "As for myself, in spite of my age, I say before God that I do not feel exempt from the obligation of laboring for the salvation of those poor people, for what could hinder me from doing so? If I cannot preach every day, all right! I will preach twice a week. If I cannot preach more important sermons, I will strive to preach less important ones; and if the people do not hear me, then what is there to prevent me from speaking in a friendly, homely way to those poor folk, as I am now speaking to you, gathering them around me as you are now" (SV XI, 136)?

My sisters, I conclude today with the words of Saint Vincent: "Charity," he tells us, "when it dwells in a soul takes complete possession of all its powers. It never rests. It is a fire that acts ceaselessly" (SV XI, 216). The Daughter of Charity is a daughter of love. She has a wonderful vocation. Saint Vincent assures her: "There is no better way to assure our eternal happiness than to live and die in the service of the poor within the arms of providence and in a real renunciation of ourselves by following Jesus Christ" (SV III, 392).

Acknowledgements

I deeply love the Vincentian heritage and fully enjoy doing research and writing about it. But I find the time to do so mainly because members of our Vincentian family urge me on. I thank them. The labor involved is rewarding for me. I hope that it is useful to the readers of this book as well.

I get lots of help! We have had wonderful secretaries here in the General Curia of the Congregation of the Mission. Let me explicitly thank Sr. Mary Ellen Sheldon and Sr. Eleanor McNabb, who served here so generously for so many years. Likewise, I am deeply grateful to the present secretarial staff, Sr. Ann Mary Dougherty (who typed and corrected the manuscript for this book), Sr. Alicia Muñoz, Mrs. Anna Carletti, and Miss Sabrina Mattiuzzo, as well as to Fr. Emeric Amyot d'Inville, the Secretary General, who coordinated their labors. Without them, this book would surely not have been written. They assist me in countless ways.